W9-CHP-669

THE
DOCTRINES
OF
Grace

THE
DOCTRINES
OF
Grace

STUDENT EDITION

SHANE LEMS

P&R PUBLISHING

P.O. BOX 817 • PHILLIPSBURG • NEW JERSEY 08865-0817

© 2013 by Shane Lems

All rights reserved. No part of this book may be reproduced, stored in a retrieval system, or transmitted in any form or by any means—electronic, mechanical, photocopy, recording, or otherwise—except for brief quotations for the purpose of review or comment, without the prior permission of the publisher, P&R Publishing Company, P.O. Box 817, Phillipsburg, New Jersey 08865-0817.

Unless otherwise indicated, Scripture quotations are from *ESV Bible* ® (*The Holy Bible, English Standard Version* ®). Copyright © 2001 by Crossway Bibles, a publishing ministry of Good News Publishers. Used by permission. All rights reserved.

Scripture references marked (NIV) are from the HOLY BIBLE, NEW INTERNATIONAL VERSION®. NIV®. Copyright © 1973, 1978, 1984 by International Bible Society. Used by permission of Zondervan Publishing House. All rights reserved.

Scripture quotations in Appendix D are taken from the King James Version.

ISBN: 978-1-59638-740-9 (pbk)
ISBN: 978-1-59638-741-6 (ePub)
ISBN: 978-1-59638-742-3 (Mobi)

Printed in the United States of America

Library of Congress Cataloging-in-Publication Data

Lems, Shane.
  The doctrines of grace / Shane Lems. -- Student Edition.
    pages cm
  Includes bibliographical references and index.
  ISBN 978-1-59638-740-9 (pbk.)
  1. Calvinism--Juvenile literature. 2. Reformed Church--Doctrines--Juvenile literature. 3. Calvinism--Textbooks. 4. Reformed Church--Doctrines--Textbooks. I. Title.
  BX9422.3.L463 2013
  230'.42--dc23
                          2013023766

I want to thank everyone who read these lessons and gave me valuable feedback (especially my wife, Lisa, and my parents). I also have to thank my catechism students who were the first ones to use these lessons. Thanks for your help, Daniel, Maisie, Ruth, Darian, and Elizabeth! Aren't you glad I never actually made you do push-ups when you forgot to do a lesson?

Finally, my thanks goes out to my Grandpa Lems, whom the Lord used to show me what perseverance of the saints looks like in real life. He read an early version of this book when he was battling cancer at the age of eighty-nine. His Christian encouragement and example are part of the reason I wrote this book.

CONTENTS

CONTENTS

A WORD TO TEACHERS AND STUDY GROUP LEADERS

Though this book could be used for individual study, it is intended for a Sunday school or church education class. If you are the leader or teacher of such a class, please realize this book is an *introduction* to the doctrines of grace (aka Calvinism or TULIP). Much more could be said about each doctrine as well as the many other doctrines of Reformed theology (covenants, church, eschatology, etc.) My goal in this book is to give the students solid biblical grounding in the doctrines of grace.

The book is divided into twelve lessons. When I used these lessons in my class, I assigned one per week. There are around ten questions for each lesson. You may want to give the students a notebook to use for answering the questions. Also, you'll notice there are two memory verses for each lesson. You can assign one or both or can even find others that fit the lesson. Appendix B shows where each doctrine is found in Reformed and Presbyterian confessions. Appendix C is a reference tool that gives Scripture references used in the book.

Finally, please look at the bibliography in appendix A. Since this book is introductory, I've given a list of other books that discuss these doctrines in more detail. Because I wanted to keep the lessons short, to the point, and easy to read, I didn't use many footnotes. However, I *did* utilize the books listed in the bibliography. I strongly recommend getting at least one or two of those books to read in preparation for teaching through this book. See appendix A for more information.

A WORD TO STUDENTS AND READERS

I'm glad you're going to read this book and use it to study. Before you start, I just want to let you know that it is an *introduction* to the doctrines of grace (aka the Five Points of Calvinism or TULIP). There is a lot more to be said about these doctrines. My main goal is to give you a basic knowledge of these doctrines and show you where they are found in the Bible. That is why each lesson has quite a few Scripture references. It is also why I gave memory verses at the end of each lesson. Appendix C has a Scripture index in case you want to look at these verses again.

I hope and pray this book will make you see the wonder and beauty of the truth that God saves sinners by grace alone. I also hope that after reading this book you want to study more about God's amazing grace in salvation. As you go through these lessons, don't forget to pray, asking God to help you learn more about his grace and love.

THE APOSTLES' CREED

I believe in God the Father, Almighty, Maker of heaven and
     earth;

And in Jesus Christ, his only begotten Son, our Lord;
     who was conceived by the Holy Spirit,
     born of the Virgin Mary,
     suffered under Pontius Pilate,
     was crucified, dead, and buried;
     he descended into hell.
     The third day he rose again from the dead.
     he ascended into heaven,
     and sits at the right hand of God the Father
     Almighty.
     From there he shall come to judge the living and
     the dead.

I believe in the Holy Spirit;
     I believe in the holy catholic (universal) church,
     the communion of saints,
     the forgiveness of sins,
     the resurrection of the body,
     and the life everlasting.
     Amen.

INTRODUCTION

STORIES . . .

The Bible is a book with many stories: the flood, the exodus, Joshua fighting the Canaanites, Samson battling the Philistines, David defeating Goliath, the prophet Hosea marrying the sinful woman, and Jesus healing the blind man. Those are just a few of the many great stories in God's Word, and I'm sure you could add more to the list.

Though there are many stories in the Bible, all of those little stories are part of one big story: our triune God saving his people from sin, death, and hell. Really, the whole Bible is this great story of God redeeming sinful people from the wages of sin, which is death (Rom. 6:23). Right at the center of this story is God's Son, Jesus. He lived, died on the cross, and rose again to save sinful people. This is what we call the *gospel*, the good news that Jesus is the Savior "who loves us and has freed us from our sins by his blood" (Rev. 1:5). The Lord himself says, "Besides me there is no savior" (Hos. 13:4). "Salvation belongs to the LORD!" (Jonah 2:9). This is also what this book is about: the saving grace of God.

In both the Old and New Testaments, this is the big story of the Bible: God the Father saves sinners through his Son Jesus by the power of his Holy Spirit. The Apostles' Creed (written on page 13) tells this story very well. Many Christians from all over the world have been saying the Apostles' Creed for around 1,500 years. All true Christians agree that the main point of the Bible is that our God saves sinners. It's what Christianity is all about!

SALVATION . . .

How exactly does God save sinners? That's a question many Christians have discussed since Augustine debated a man named Pelagius around A.D. 400. Shortly after 1500 the Protestant Reformers like Martin Luther and John Calvin wrote, preached, and talked about justification by faith alone. They strongly disagreed with the Roman Catholic Church, which said sinners are justified by grace and faith, but also by obedience to the church and God's law. The Reformers said sinners are justified by grace alone through faith alone in Christ alone. God used the Reformers to re-form the church according to his Word, the Bible.

HISTORY . . .

In the early 1600s some people in the Reformed churches of Holland were saying things about salvation that didn't sound Reformed or biblical. These people, called the Remonstrants or Arminians, summarized their teaching with five points. This is what they taught:

1. All people have free will, which means they can either choose to believe in Jesus or choose not to believe in him.

16

2. Before the world began, God elected (chose to save) people whom he knew would use their free will to believe in Jesus.

3. Jesus died to make salvation possible for anyone who uses his or her free will to believe in him.

4. The Holy Spirit draws people to Jesus, but people can use their free will to resist the Holy Spirit.

5. Someone who is truly a Christian can fall away and not be a Christian anymore.

This is a short summary; we'll talk more about these things later.

Many pastors and elders in Holland strongly disagreed with these five points. A church meeting (called a synod) was held in the city of Dordrecht in 1618. Pastors and elders from Holland (and several from other countries) talked about these five points in the meeting. After much discussion, study of Scripture, and prayer, the Synod came up with five points of its own. Their five points showed that the Arminians' five points were neither Reformed nor biblical. They wrote a church document called the Canons of Dort. Solid Reformed churches still appreciate, preach, and teach these truths today. Later in this book we will refer to the Canons of Dort. You can find the Canons in appendix D.

➥ A *canon* is a statement.
➥ *Dort* is short for the city of Dordrecht.

CHURCHES . . .

It is also important to know that the Canons of Dort teach basically the same things as other Reformed documents like the Heidelberg Catechism and the Belgic Confession of Faith. The Presbyterian documents—the Westminster Confession and Catechisms—also teach the same things as the Canons of Dort. But the Canons of Dort speak only about the doctrines of grace specifically, while the other confessions deal with many more biblical topics. The point is that these confessions stand together on the main truths of the Christian faith. Presbyterian and Reformed churches that use these documents (also called confessions) are in agreement on these five points of the Canons of Dort. (Look at appendix B for more information on this.) Of course there is a lot more to being Reformed than just these five points. These five points aren't the only things Reformed Christians believe. But they are an important part of Reformation teaching.

➲ *Confessions* are statements of faith.

TULIP . . .

Most people know these five points as the five points of Calvinism. The popular acronym is TULIP, which stands for this:

1. Total depravity
2. Unconditional election
3. Limited atonement
4. Irresistible grace
5. Perseverance of the saints

Usually, if someone is a *Calvinist*, he or she believes these doctrines of grace are biblical. But I don't think we should use the name *Calvinist*, since John Calvin himself would not like us to think he made up these points. Many in the Christian church believed and taught these truths before Calvin was even alive. A better name for these points is *the doctrines of grace*. That's why the title of this book is what it is.

THIS BOOK . . .

In this book we will see how these doctrines have everything to do with God's grace. Pay attention to the following lessons. We're going to look at many Bible verses that talk about grace and salvation from sin. Each lesson will also have two memory verses. One goal of this book is to learn and memorize what the Bible says about salvation from sin. Another goal I have in writing this book is to show how these doctrines of grace are meaningful in the Christian life. They aren't just truths for the Christian mind. They are also truths for the Christian heart. People who believe these doctrines of grace should live joy-filled, thankful Christian lives of obedience to God.

In this book there are twelve lessons: an introduction lesson (which you're reading right now), a concluding lesson, and two lessons on each of the five doctrines of grace. This book is only an introduction to the doctrines of grace, so we won't be discussing all the details. Appendix A has a list of books that are good ones for further study—many of which I've used to write this book. Appendix C has a list of all the Bible verses this book uses to explain the doctrines of grace.

STUDY QUESTIONS

1. What are some of your favorite stories in the Bible?
2. What is the main story of the Bible?

3. What is the gospel?
4. Read the Apostles' Creed on page 13. Do you think it is a good summary of the main story of the Bible? Why or why not?
5. What is one thing the Protestant Reformers emphasized, and why did they emphasize it so much?
6. What are the five points that the Arminians taught in the early 1600s?
7. Briefly explain the Synod of Dordrecht and the Canons of Dort.
8. What does TULIP stand for?
9. Do you think *Calvinism* is a good name for these five points? Why or why not?
10. What are the two goals of this book?
11. Do you think Christian doctrine is something that will help Christians in their daily lives? Explain.

MEMORY WORK

Salvation belongs to the LORD! (Jonah 2:9)

I am the LORD your God . . . besides me there is no savior. (Hos. 13:4)

HOW SINFUL ARE PEOPLE?

CLEARLY . . .

There are many things the Bible clearly teaches. For example, the Bible teaches the God of Abraham, Isaac, and Jacob made all things out of nothing (Gen. 1:1; Ps. 33:9; John 1:1–3; etc.). The Bible also teaches that God is still in control of all things (Ps. 104; Matt. 6:26–30; Heb. 1:3; etc.). He is the only true and living God (1 Kings 8:60). There is no other god (Isa. 45:5).

> ➲ The *will* is the part of us that makes decisions.

Another thing the Bible clearly teaches is that Adam and Eve were created "very good" and in God's image. They were righteous and holy (Gen. 1:31; Eph. 4:24). The Canons of Dort say that man's "heart and will were upright, all his affections pure, and the whole man was holy" (III/IV, article 1). Adam and Eve had free will to choose good or evil.

However, they chose evil by eating the fruit God had told them not to eat. They sinned (Gen. 2). Because of Adam's disobedience, sin and death came into the world (Rom. 5:12). Adam's sin "led to condemnation for all men . . . by the one man's disobedience the many were made sinners" (Rom. 5:18–19). Because of Adam's sin, all people are conceived in sin (Ps. 51:5). "Man after the fall begat children in his own likeness" (Canons III/IV, article 2). Some people say children learn to sin by imitating sinful people around them. But the Bible says children are sinful from conception. Sinful parents have sinful children. This is what we call *original sin*.

◆ *Conceived* means the beginning of a pregnancy.

SINFUL . . .

The question we have to ask is, "How sinful are people?" How badly did Adam's fall hurt his children and his children's children? The Bible paints a dark picture of the sinfulness of human beings. Before the flood the Bible says man was so sinful that "every intention of the thoughts of his heart was only evil continually" (Gen. 6:5). Ecclesiastes 9:3 says, "The hearts of the children of man are full of evil." The prophet Jeremiah told God's people that "the heart is deceitful above all things, and desperately sick; who can understand it?" (17:9). The Bible is so clear on the sinfulness of humanity it says, "No one living is righteous" (Ps. 143:2; see also Eccl. 7:20). Even people's minds are darkened by sin (Eph. 4:18).

What this means is that people are not good deep down inside. Sometimes we hear speeches on the radio, Internet, or TV about the basic goodness of humanity. However, the Bible teaches the exact opposite. Since Adam sinned, all humans are sinful people deep down. The deeper you go inside, the uglier people get (Mark 7:21–23). Other Bible words for sinfulness are iniquity, corruption, wickedness, evil, rebellion, malice, and transgression. This is what the *T* of TULIP stands for: total depravity.

TOTAL . . .

These words, *total depravity*, mean that every part of a person has been messed up by sin. A person's body, soul, mind, will, words, thoughts, desires, and deeds are twisted by sin. People think sinful thoughts. They say sinful words. They have hatred in their hearts. People even use their bodies to do terrible things like fight and kill.

Paul says it pretty sharply: people are "children of wrath" (Eph. 2:3). Wicked leaders like Adolf Hitler and Osama bin Laden showed how sinful humanity can be. But we don't have to look too far away to see terrible sinfulness. Our own towns have police officers to stop people from drunk driving, stealing, and killing. Sometimes in our hearts we show our own terrible sinfulness when we hate someone and wish he or she were dead. The great king David didn't just lie, he also murdered, committed adultery, and broke many of the Ten Commandments!

Total depravity doesn't mean that every person is as bad as he or she could possibly be. God is sovereign (Isa. 46:10–11). He doesn't allow the world to be taken over by murderers and thieves. Sometimes he destroys wicked rulers like Pharaoh and Herod. Other times God uses rulers like the Queen of Sheba, Cyrus, and Nebuchadnezzar to help his people (Ex. 14; 1 Kings 10; Ezra 1; Dan. 3; Acts 12:23).

➲ *Sovereign* means to have total power and control.

Though sin has almost wrecked the image of God in people, in some way every person still has some decency left. People may sometimes act like animals, but sin doesn't make us actual animals. The Canons of Dort explain it this way: "There remain . . . in man since the fall, the glimmerings of natural light, whereby he retains some knowledge of God, of natural things, and of the differences between good and evil, and discovers some regard for virtue" (III/IV, article 4). In other words, though God's image and goodness is shattered, there are some glimmers of it left in people.

The Bible talks about this in Romans 2:15. Paul says that in some way all people's hearts and consciences know God's law. Of course this doesn't mean that all people are Christians. It means people generally know that killing is a bad thing and helping someone is a good thing.

IN OTHER WORDS . . .

Another way to talk about total depravity is to say that depravity is extensive and not intensive. This just means that sinfulness *extends* to the whole person (heart, soul, body, mind). But people's sinfulness isn't as *intense* as it could be. They could be a lot more sinful than they actually are!

The doctrine of total depravity explains why there are robberies, racists, abortions, murders, wars, and other sorts of evil. In this world, there *is* such a thing as sin, wickedness, and disobedience to God. The Bible teaches about sin very clearly. This might not be a new teaching to you, but remember that not very many people today say that sin is the main problem in the world. Christians are the only people who take sin very seriously. We call it what it is.

24

If we don't understand what the Bible says about sin, we won't understand what the Bible says about salvation from sin. When we say that Jesus is the Savior of sinners, we mean that Jesus is the Savior of evil, wicked, nasty, God-hating people who deserve to be punished forever for their sins (Rom. 5:6, 8; 1 Cor. 6:9).

Jesus didn't come to help people be better. Jesus didn't come to show good people the right way to live. He came to save wicked people by taking away their sins through his death on the cross (Mark 2:17; Col. 2:14). Jesus took the punishment that his people deserve and gave them gifts they didn't deserve: forgiveness and eternal life (2 Cor. 5:21). That is why Paul calls Christ's work the good news, or "the gospel" (1 Cor. 15:1–3). The name *Jesus* itself is good news because it means "he will save his people from their sins" (Matt. 1:21). We can also say Jesus' name tells us of God's amazing grace.

STUDY QUESTIONS

1. Besides the examples in this lesson, what are some things the Bible clearly teaches? List three.
2. Do children sin *only* because they learn to sin by watching other people sin? Explain your answer using the Bible.
3. What is original sin?
4. Write out four Bible verses that explain how sinful (depraved) people are.
5. When you see evil and sin in the world today, does it make you think of total depravity? Explain.
6. Does total depravity mean people are as sinful as they possibly could be? Explain.
7. What does it mean to say God is sovereign?

8. What does God's sovereignty mean in your own life?

9. Do all people know God's law at least to some extent? Read Romans 2:15 and give your answer.

10. If we don't understand what the Bible teaches about sin, what other teachings of the Bible will we mess up?

11. For whom did Jesus die: decent people trying hard to be good or wicked sinners on their way to hell? Explain your answer with Bible verses.

12. How can the doctrine of total depravity keep you humble and not arrogant?

13. What do these words, "Jesus died to save sinners," mean for you when you feel like a failure?

MEMORY WORK

The heart is deceitful above all things, and desperately sick; who can understand it? (Jer. 17:9)

None is righteous, no, not one; no one understands; no one seeks for God. (Rom. 3:10–11)

SLAVES OF SIN

REVIEW . . .

In the last lesson we learned what total depravity means. All people are conceived and born in sin. Every part of every person is sinful. Though nobody is as terrible as he or she could be, all people break God's law by nature. People aren't basically decent people. They're sinful deep down. "No one does good, not even one" (Rom. 3:12).

SLAVERY . . .

The Bible teaches another thing about sin that is very important for us to know: "Everyone who sins is a slave to sin" (John 8:34 NIV). This has to do with total depravity. Because of Adam's sin, because we're conceived in sin, and because we actually do sinful things, we are in bondage to sin. By nature people are "neither able nor willing to return to God, to reform the depravity of their nature, nor to dispose themselves to reformation" (Canons III/IV, article 3). People aren't forced to sin. They sin because they're sinful deep down.

This means that we do not have the power to escape the bondage of sin. Sinful people cannot do anything to help themselves "get saved" from sin. Martin Luther wrote a book in 1525 called *The Bondage of the Will*. That title is another way to say what the Bible teaches about sin. Augustine wrote in 420 that after Adam sinned in the garden, "the freedom of his will was lost." It makes us think of Acts 8:23 where Paul told Simon the sorcerer that sin held him captive.

IN OTHER WORDS . . .

There are quite a few other biblical ways to explain this slavery. The Bible says people are dead in sin (Eph. 2:1). Paul reminded Titus that they were both once slaves to sinful passions and wicked pleasures (Titus 3:3). Paul also reminded the Christians in Rome that they used to be "slaves of sin" (Rom. 6:20). Back in the days of the prophets in Israel, Jeremiah told the people that it was impossible for them to stop doing evil and start doing good (Jer. 13:23).

⬌ The Bible says people are *dead in sin*.

Jesus also said that it is impossible for a bad tree to produce good fruit. A sinful heart cannot produce deeds that are good in God's eyes (Matt. 7:16–18). Unbelievers cannot use their free will to believe in Jesus whenever they want. Total depravity also means humans are totally unable to chose what is spiritually good. Total depravity and total inability (or bondage of the will) go together very closely. The Reformers argued with the Roman Catholic Church on this point, since Rome said that people are partly depraved and still have free will left. Arminians say almost the same thing.

Another way to talk about bondage of the will is to say that people are not just sick with sin. Sin isn't a disease or a sickness. It means spiritual deadness. Someone who is not a Christian is so stuck in sin he or she cannot please God at all (Rom. 8:8). In the Bible, Jesus told the Pharisees that the Devil was their father (John 8:44). John wrote that Cain (way back in Genesis) "was of the evil one" (1 John 3:10, 12). The Westminster Larger Catechism says we are by nature "bond slaves to Satan" (Q/A 27). A person stuck in sin is under the tyranny of Satan.

➡ *Tyranny* means wicked rule.

ILLUSTRATION . . .

Think of a prisoner. If someone is in jail, she can eat with other prisoners, wake up in the morning, and get sunshine when she is allowed. But she's stuck in prison and can't get out. She's in bondage. She can't undo her crime. She can't change the judge's guilty verdict. She can't clear her record, and she can't make her record good. In one sense she has some freedom, but really she's in prison with a guilty verdict hanging over her head.

People do have the freedom to pick which pair of socks they will wear for the day. People also can think for themselves and decide to give a meal to a homeless man if they want. When we talk about total depravity and bondage of the will, we're not saying that people can't make normal daily decisions.

What we are saying—based on Bible teaching—is that nobody has the ability to make himself or herself acceptable to God by choosing what is good in his sight. Everyone has the ability to do certain daily things, but nobody has the ability to decide to become a Christian. The problem is not that we're humans. The problem is that we're terribly *sinful* humans. The problem is that we are completely trapped in sin. The problem is that it is impossible for a person to choose to do what is truly good in God's eyes.

STORY . . .

I remember the story of a seminary professor who took his preaching class to a cemetery and told them to start preaching to the dead bodies buried in the ground. The students were confused but did what the professor said (even though they really didn't want to!).

The professor later told them that's what it's like when an unbeliever hears the gospel. The dead person can't get up and believe, and the preacher can't make a dead person get up and believe. The only one who can do that is God. We'll talk about that more in the lessons on irresistible grace. For now remember that by nature all people are in bondage to sin.

◆ By nature all people are in bondage to sin.

SUMMARY OF TOTAL DEPRAVITY (LESSONS 2-3) . . .

God created man good and in his own image. Man disobeyed God and now the whole human race is very sinful. All humans are in the prison of sin and unable to get out on their own. In fact, many people don't realize it and many other people don't even care. Some people even love to sin! I once read how some Nazis in WWII laughed when Jews died right in front of them. Evil is real and powerful, and it holds many people captive.

But just because all people are in this prison of sin doesn't mean there is no hope. Thankfully God is merciful, kind, and loving. He has decided to save some sinners, even though they deserve to be lost forever. We'll talk about amazing grace in the lessons to come. The important thing to remember is that nobody deserves to be saved from sin, death, and hell, because "all have sinned and fall short of the glory of God" (Rom. 3:23). The Canons of Dort start on this biblical point: God would have done no injustice by letting everyone die in their sin. We must never forget that if we want to understand the "amazingness" of grace.

STUDY QUESTIONS

1. For review, define total depravity.
2. What was the title of Martin Luther's book that he wrote in 1525? What does it have to do with this lesson?
3. In this lesson we learned that Paul told Titus and the church in Rome that before they were Christians they were . . . (finish the sentence). Is any sinner too sinful to be saved?
4. What did Jesus mean by the fruit tree illustration in Matthew 7:16–18?
5. What did we learn about Satan in this lesson?
6. Is it okay for us to hate sin, evil, and Satan? Explain.
7. Do people have some amount of freedom? Explain.
8. Explain the story of the seminary students preaching in the cemetery.
9. Based on this lesson, define bondage of the will (total inability) in two or three sentences.

10. Read the first sentence of the Canons of Dort and write it down in your own words.
11. Is there any hope for people who are dead in sin? Explain.
12. What does it mean for you to have hope even though you still struggle with sin?

MEMORY WORK

A healthy tree cannot bear bad fruit, nor can a diseased tree bear good fruit. (Matt. 7:18)

For we ourselves were once foolish, disobedient, led astray, slaves to various passions and pleasures, passing our days in malice and envy, hated by others and hating one another. (Titus 3:3)

A COMMUNITY CHOSEN

When we use the term *election* in Christianity, we are not talking about voting in November. Instead, *election* is the term used in the Bible to describe God choosing to save people even before he created the world. *Elect* means to choose to save. Other biblical words like election are *chosen* and *predestined*.

➲ *Elect* means to choose to save.

Ephesians 1 teaches very clearly that God chose his people "before the foundation of the world . . . In love he predestined us for adoption as sons through Jesus Christ, according to the purpose of his will" (1:4–5). Later in Ephesians 1, Paul says that Christians "have been predestined according to the purpose of him who works all things according to the counsel of his will" (1:11). If you read Ephesians 1, you will see that the Bible does teach election.

Other places in the Bible also teach election. Jesus spoke about the elect (Matt. 24:22–24, 31; Mark 13:20–22, 27). Jesus also said to his disciples, "You did not choose me, but I chose you" and "I know whom I have chosen" (John 13:18; 15:16). Many of us have heard these words of Jesus: "Many are called, but few are chosen" (Matt. 22:14).

The Old Testament also talks about election. Psalm 33:12 says that the people whom God has *chosen* as his heritage are blessed (see also Ps. 65:4; 106:5). Israel was God's chosen nation in the Old Testament (Deut. 7:6; Isa. 44:1). Later we'll talk about other places in the Bible that talk about predestination and election.

➲ The Old Testament also talks about election.

REFORMED . . .

If we want to follow the Bible's teaching about God saving sinners, we do have to say this: yes, even before he created the world, God did choose to save sinners. Because election is taught in the Bible, the Reformed and Presbyterian confessions also teach it. The Heidelberg Catechism says that God's people are "a community chosen for eternal life" (Q/A 54). The Canons of Dort explain election as God's unchangeable purpose of choosing a certain number of fallen sinners. He elected them before creating the world (I, article 7). The Westminster Confession says very much the same thing.

We shouldn't be afraid to use the words *elect* and *predestined* since they are used in the Bible. Even if some of our Christian friends never heard of election before, or if some of them do not like this teaching, we can use these words because the Bible uses them.

CAREFUL . . .

When we do talk about election, we should be very careful not to say more about it than the Bible says. The Bible does teach that God has chosen people to be saved from sin. But if we say more than the Bible says, we are sinning. John Calvin said that going beyond what the Bible says about election is like going down a terrible, dark maze that is almost impossible to escape.[1] In other words, we don't want to do it!

⮕ We should never say more about election than the Bible says about it.

We also have to be careful not to view everything in terms of election. We can't go around thinking, "That person is probably not elect" or "I wonder if she's elect." The Canons of Dort tell us that we shouldn't try to explore "the secret ways" of God (I, article 14). In other words, election is God's business and not ours. He knows all about it; we know very little. He knows all the names written in the book of life, but we don't (Rev. 20:15; 21:27).

We do know for sure that God hasn't elected every person who ever lived. For example, God condemned and destroyed the cities of Sodom and Gomorrah for their wickedness (Gen. 18–19). Judas was "the one doomed to destruction" (John 17:12 NIV). God said Esau was not elect (Rom. 9:10–13). There is such a thing as hell, which Paul calls "eternal destruction" (2 Thess. 1:9). The Bible teaches that God chose to save some people but not everyone. He is sovereign. He does what pleases him.

---

1. John Calvin, *Institutes of the Christian Religion* (Louisville: Westminster John Knox, 1960), III.XXI.1.

Another way to say it is that God chose to save some but passed by others. God leaves some in the "common misery" of their sin (Canons I, article 15). He leaves them alone because of their unbelief and sin. This is also called *reprobation*. God is just. Those who are not elect are punished for their sins. God doesn't punish people who believe in him and love him. He punishes sinners who reject and hate him. Paul calls the reprobate "vessels of wrath prepared for destruction" (Rom. 9:22).

➲ *Reprobate* means not elect.

Here we have to be very careful once again. We can say that Jacob was elect and Esau was not elect (or reprobate) because the Bible says it (Rom. 9:10–13). But we can't really speak about it much more than that. Reprobation is God's business and not ours. Like Paul says, God's ways are beyond us and impossible for us to figure out (Rom. 11:33). What God doesn't tell us we should never try to figure out. Psalm 147:5 tells us that God's "understanding is beyond measure."

We have to talk about one more thing before we end this lesson. God doesn't force people to sin. He doesn't tempt people to sin (James 1:13). God is not the author or maker of sin. He hates sin (Prov. 6:16; Zech. 8:17). But he does allow it and uses it for his purpose (Gen. 50:20; Acts 2:23). God is sovereign. Sin does not ruin his plans.

FINALLY . . .

When we think about election, we have to remember that God is sovereign. God would still be God without people. He doesn't need us. God doesn't owe anybody anything (Rom. 9:18). He could have chosen to save every sinner. Or he could have chosen to save nobody. In his freedom, justice, and mercy he chose to save some and not others. He loved and chose Jacob but not Esau (Rom. 9:13). It's up to him, not us. We can't say it's not fair, because everyone deserves to be punished for his or her sin.

This has to do with grace again. To think that God actually chose to save some sinful people is amazing. All people deserve to be punished forever for their sin, but God decided to save some and give them eternal life. That's amazing grace and mercy!

This teaching should make Christians "adore the depth" of God's mercies (Canons I, article 13). It should also excite us to worship God more for his great love toward us. "In this is love, not that we have loved God but that he loved us and sent his Son to be the propitiation for our sins" (1 John 4:10).

Before we go on to do the questions, remember this. Believing in election does not save us. Election did not die on the cross for us. Jesus did. Believe in the Lord Jesus Christ and you will be saved (Acts 16:31)! We don't have to climb up to heaven to see if we're elect. We simply have to bow down before God, repent, and believe in Jesus.

STUDY QUESTIONS

1. What does *elect* mean?
2. Write the words in Ephesians 1:3–6 that have to do with election.
3. Does the Old Testament talk about election? Prove it.
4. Does the Bible teach *all* the details of election? What does that mean when we study it?

5. Has God chosen to save every person who ever lived? Prove your answer.

6. What does *reprobate* mean?

7. What does God think about sin? See Proverbs 6:16.

8. The lesson said that sin does not ruin God's plans. What does that mean for your Christian life?

9. True or false: God was forced to elect some sinners. Explain your answer.

10. What would you say to someone who doesn't like the word *election* or *predestination*?

MEMORY WORK

In love he predestined us for adoption as sons through Jesus Christ, according to the purpose of his will. (Eph. 1:4–5)

[God said] I will have mercy on whom I have mercy, and I will have compassion on whom I have compassion. (Rom. 9:15)

WHY AND WHEN?

REVIEW . . .

In the last lesson we talked about election. Election means that before he created the world God decided to save some sinful people. He also passed by some and left them in their sin. Nobody deserves to be chosen by God because "all have sinned and fall short of the glory of God" (Rom. 3:23). God is just in punishing sinners for their sin. God is merciful and gracious for electing to save some from their sin.

ELECTION . . .

There is one huge question we have to ask: why did God choose some people? Arminians teach that God elected people who he knew would believe in him. They say God looked ahead in time and knew everyone who would have faith. Those are the people he chose to save. In other words, election depends on a person's faith.

This is called *conditional election* because it makes election conditional on a person's faith. Another way to think about it is someone getting paid for doing a job. Payment is conditional on doing the job. If you do the job, you get paid. Arminians say that election is conditional on faith. They say God chose people who chose him first. Election is based on a person's choice.

➲ *Conditional* means to depend on something.

Reformed Christians strongly disagree with the Arminian teaching of election. The Canons of Dort and the Westminster Confession of Faith teach that God chose people based on his own mercy. God didn't elect sinners because he knew they would believe. He elected them because he loved them. God chose people before they chose him. Election is based on God's choice, not any human's.

UNCONDITIONAL . . .

This is called *unconditional election*. Here's where we get the *U* in TULIP. *Unconditional* means that election doesn't depend on something we do. "Election was not founded on foreseen faith" (Canons I, article 9). Election depends completely on God's sovereign mercy and love. It is not conditional on something we do.

➲ Election is not conditional on something we do.

Remember what we learned about total depravity. Every part of every person is messed up with sin. Every person is stuck in sin and unable to choose to do good things that please God. God elected to save some of these sinners. He didn't choose them because they were decent people. They weren't. They were sinners completely dead in sin. They didn't have the power or desire to believe. He chose them because he is a loving and merciful God. That is why the Canons of Dort call this "gracious election" (I, article 10). It is based on grace, not on something people do.

SCRIPTURE . . .

What is most important here is what the Bible says about election. We already learned that the Bible *does* teach election. Now let's look at some verses that talk about unconditional election.

In the last lesson, we talked about Ephesians 1. There Paul says that God chose his people "before the foundation of the world, that we should be holy and blameless before him" (v. 4). He didn't choose his people *because* they were holy or blameless. He chose them *so that* they would be holy and blameless. Paul also said that God predestined his people "according to the purpose of his will" (v. 5). He predestined them not because of their will or choice, but because of his will and choice.

We should also think about Abraham and his children. We know that God chose Abraham when Abraham was an unbeliever in a foreign nation (Gen. 11:31–12:4). In Romans 9 Paul talks about Abraham's twin grandsons, Jacob and Esau. Paul says that before the twins were born, before they did anything good or bad, God elected Jacob. Look at Paul's own words:

> Though they were not yet born and had done nothing either good or bad—in order that God's purpose of election might

41

continue, not because of works but because of his call—she [Rebekah] was told, "The older will serve the younger." (Rom. 9:11–12)

God didn't choose Jacob because of something Jacob did. Election was not conditional on Jacob's faith or will. Election depends on God's purpose, choice, and will. Election depends on God's grace. That is why Paul says people are "chosen by grace" (Rom. 11:5–6). Paul himself knew this well. He was on his way to hurt Christians in Damascus when Jesus changed his wicked heart. Jesus called Paul his "chosen instrument" (Acts 9:15). Jesus chose Paul before Paul chose Jesus!

Another story is important. In Acts 13 we read about Paul and Barnabas preaching about Jesus in Antioch. After they preached, the Bible says, "As many as were appointed to eternal life believed" (v. 48). God didn't appoint them to eternal life because they believed. They believed because they were appointed to eternal life, which means elected.

Election also has to do with providence. God is in control of everything. He has a purpose and plan that he is carrying out. "'My counsel shall stand, and I will accomplish all my purpose' . . . I have purposed, I will do it" (Isa. 46:10–11). His plan includes saving the people whom he chose.

➲ Election also has to do with providence.

DON'T FORGET . . .

We also have to remember that election has everything to do with Jesus. We can never talk about election without talking about Jesus. God "predestined us for adoption as sons through Jesus Christ, according to the purpose of his will" (Eph. 1:5). We'll talk more about this later. For now just remember that God chose to save sinful people. Jesus is the Savior of sinners. God's plan of salvation is the main message of the Bible.

Unconditional election is not the easiest thing in the Bible to study. When we study this we have to remember that God is God. He is the potter and we are the clay (Rom. 9:21). He does his will. He does what brings himself glory. He doesn't make mistakes. Even though we don't totally understand this, we know that God is sovereign. Not even Paul completely understood all the details of election. That is why he wrote a deep hymn after he talked about election and reprobation (Rom. 11:33–36). Read that now because you'll have to answer a question about it later.

SUMMARY OF UNCONDITIONAL ELECTION . . .

Let's review. The Bible teaches election. In his mercy God chose to save some people from sin and hell. In his justice he passed by other sinners and left them in their sin. Since all people are sinful, nobody deserves to be chosen and saved. We don't know all the details of election and reprobation. But we do know that God is the Judge of all the earth and he does what is just (Gen. 18:25). He has mercy on whom he wants to have mercy (Ex. 33:19)

This biblical teaching of unconditional election is not just something to learn and forget about. It is something that matters in our everyday Christian life. It keeps us humble, because we don't know everything. But we do know we've been elected and saved by grace, not by what we do. We don't deserve to be chosen, but since God is merciful, he elects and saves his people. This also leads us to love him and praise him! We can live each day with joy and thankfulness knowing that he loved us and gave his Son to die for us.

STUDY QUESTIONS

1. For review, explain how God is merciful and just in election and reprobation.
2. What is conditional election?
3. What is unconditional election? (This is the *U* in TULIP.)
4. This lesson mentioned total depravity again. What does unconditional election have to do with total depravity?
5. Whose will is ultimate in election? Read Ephesians 1:5.
6. Did God elect Jacob because of Jacob's faith? Prove it.
7. What does it mean that we're chosen by grace and not works? Does this encourage you in your Christian faith? How?
8. How do providence and election go together?
9. Can we talk about election without mentioning Jesus? Explain.
10. Read Romans 11:33–36. Explain how election leads the Christian to worship the Lord.

MEMORY WORK

So then it depends not on human will or exertion, but on God, who has mercy. (Rom. 9:16)

And when the Gentiles heard this, they began rejoicing and glorifying the word of the Lord, and as many as were appointed to eternal life believed. (Acts 13:48)

MISSION ACCOMPLISHED

T he next doctrine of grace we are going to study has to do with the main story of the Bible. Earlier we learned that the main story of the Bible is Jesus saving totally depraved sinners. That's the good news. Jesus saves! God is merciful, kind, and loving. He sent his Son to rescue us from sin, death, and hell, even though we don't deserve it.

So far we've learned about *T* (total depravity) and *U* (unconditional election). Now we're up to the *L*. *L* stands for limited atonement. Before we talk about the meaning of *limited*, we have to talk about the word *atonement*.

ATONEMENT . . .

The first place to find atonement in the Bible is Exodus 29–30. There we learn that atonement had to do with sacrificing an animal. Leviticus 4 also mentions atonement. In Leviticus 4:26 *atonement* means that a sacrifice was killed and a person's sins were forgiven. The Bible's teaching is that a sacrificed animal took the place of sinful people. People deserve to die for their sins. But God in his goodness said a sacrifice would turn away his wrath against sin. Sacrifices in the Old Testament showed that God deals with sin and forgives it at the same time.

Atonement has to do with (1) sacrifice, (2) the forgiveness of sins, and (3) the turning away of God's wrath against sin. We won't go through all the details, but remember the lesson on total depravity. All people are sinful and deserve to be punished forever by God for their sins. This has been true since Adam's sin in the garden. The sacrifices in the Old Testament were signs or arrows that reminded the people that sins could be forgiven through a bloody death.

The New Testament tells us that Jesus' sacrifice and death is the final sacrifice for sin. All the sacrificed animals of the Old Testament pointed forward to Jesus. The whole book of Hebrews talks about Jesus' sacrifice as the only thing that can take away our sin. The Bible also says Jesus' death was substitutionary (Isa. 53:5–6). In other words, he took the place of sinners when he died on the cross (Gal. 3:13). "Christ loved us and gave himself up for us, a . . . sacrifice to God" (Eph. 5:2).

➲ The Old Testament sacrifices point forward to Jesus' death on the cross.

The Canons of Dort remind us that we are unable to "deliver ourselves from the wrath of God" (II, article 2). In his love God sent his Son to atone for the sins of his people (1 John 4:10). This is the gospel, the good news. "Christ also suffered once for sins, the righteous for the unrighteous, that he might bring us to God" (1 Peter 3:18).

VALUABLE . . .

Jesus' death on the cross has so much value. It means victory over sin, death, Satan, and hell (1 Cor. 15:55). It means the forgiveness of sins (Col. 1:14). Jesus' sacrifice means God's anger against sin is turned away and the curse is gone (Rom. 5:9; Gal. 3:13). It means sinful people can be justified (Rom. 5:9). It means God and sinners can be friends instead of enemies (2 Cor. 5:19). Jesus' death means God's people are called his adopted children (1 John 3:1). It also means that Christians have eternal life (1 John 5:11). The word *limited* in TULIP doesn't have to do with the value of Jesus' death. Jesus' death is valuable for us in more ways than we can count!

➡ *Justified* means declared righteous by God.

The Bible uses a lot of words to describe the awesome things Jesus did for us in his death and resurrection. These are some words the Bible uses: reconciliation, propitiation, ransom, redemption, and atonement. The Canons of Dort tell us that Jesus' death is of "infinite worth and value" (II, article 3). Jesus' death and resurrection is the only thing that can save sinners from hell. And it is the only thing we need! When we believe in Jesus, God justifies us. He takes away all our sin and gives us all the blessings Jesus gained for us in his death.

AGREEMENT . . .

All Christians agree that Jesus is the only Savior (Acts 4:12). All Christians agree that whoever truly believes in Jesus is saved (Eph. 2:8). And as we learned earlier, all good Christians agree that not everybody is going to be saved. There is a place the Bible calls hell (Matt. 23:33; 25:41). This is the place of eternal punishment for people who don't repent and believe in Jesus.

DISAGREEMENT . . .

There is some disagreement on the topic of the atonement. Arminian Christians say that Jesus died to make salvation possible for anyone. They say that Jesus' goal on the cross was to open the door of salvation. This is called unlimited atonement. Unlimited atonement means Jesus' atonement is not limited to certain people. The design of Jesus' death was to make salvation a possibility for everyone. One other way to say it is like this: the atonement made salvation possible for everyone if they believe in Jesus.

Reformed Christians disagree. We state that Jesus actually accomplished salvation by his death and resurrection. His atonement was definite. He definitely saved his people when he died for them. Jesus' goal was to save people by his death. He achieved that goal when he died and rose again.

➡ The only redeemer of God's elect is the Lord Jesus Christ.

The Canons of Dort say that the salvation Jesus accomplished on the cross extends "to all the elect" (II, article 8). The Westminster Shorter Catechism tells us that "the only Redeemer of God's elect is the Lord Jesus Christ" (Q/A 21). This is called *limited* atonement because Jesus' death secured salvation for a limited number of people. He didn't secure salvation for everyone. Therefore we can also call it *particular redemption* or *definite atonement*.

SUMMARY . . .

In the next lesson we'll talk about this some more. For now, remember what atonement means. It means that on the cross Jesus died to save sinners. He took their place and he took their punishment. The result is amazing. Jesus' death means sinful people who believe in him are loved, justified, accepted, forgiven, reconciled, and given eternal life. Again, this is the gospel, the good news of amazing grace. Maybe we should call this book the doctrines of *amazing* grace!

As you look ahead to the next lesson, think about these questions: Did Jesus die to make salvation possible, or did he die to actually save sinful people? Is Jesus possibly a Savior of sinners or is he really and actually a Savior?

According to the doctrines of grace, Jesus is a real Savior who really saved his people by dying for them on the cross. He accomplished his mission of saving his people. In the next lesson we'll study some Bible verses that show this truth. One to think of for now is found in Ephesians 5:25: "Christ loved the church and gave himself up for her."

STUDY QUESTIONS

1. Read Leviticus 4:26. What does it say about atonement and sin?
2. To what did the Old Testament sacrifices point?
3. Atonement has to do with three things. What are they?
4. Jesus died as our substitute. What does that mean as you think about your own sinfulness?

5. Name some things that Jesus' death means for Christians.
6. Arminians believe Jesus' death made salvation POSSIBLE or ACTUAL. (Circle one.)
7. Reformed Christians believe Jesus' death made salvation POSSIBLE or ACTUAL. (Circle one.)
8. What is unlimited atonement?
9. What is limited atonement?
10. Does the teaching of limited atonement bring spiritual comfort to the Christian? Explain.

MEMORY WORK

Christ also suffered once for sins, the righteous for the unrighteous, that he might bring us to God. (1 Peter 3:18)

Christ loved the church and gave himself up for her. (Eph. 5:25)

CHAPTER 7

DID JESUS FAIL?

REVIEW . . .

We're still talking about Christ's atonement in this lesson. Through Christ's sacrifice, believing sinners are forgiven because God's wrath has been turned away. We learned that in our last lesson. We also learned the difference between unlimited atonement and limited (or definite) atonement. Let's quickly summarize the differences, and then we'll study some Bible verses.

Arminians say that Jesus' death unlocked the door of our prison cells. All that we have to do is open the door by our faith. In Arminian teaching, Christ is like a lifeguard who throws a rope out for people who are drowning. All they have to do is grab the rope. In other words, Jesus' death didn't definitely save people. His death just made it possible for people to be saved. That's a summary of unlimited atonement.

But according to the doctrines of grace (TULIP), Christ's atonement actually saved people. Jesus' death unlocked the door of our prison cells. But he didn't stop there. He went into the cells of his people and brought them all the way out.

Calvinists teach that Christ is like a lifeguard who jumps in the water, grabs people who have drowned, brings them to shore, and breathes life into them. Jesus' death actually saved the elect. It didn't just make salvation possible. This is called limited, or definite, atonement.

◆ Christ's atonement actually saved people.

BIBLE STUDY . . .

Whatever the Bible teaches about Christ's atonement is right. We want to do our best to learn what the Bible says. Now we're going to spend time looking at some verses and teachings of the Bible that have to do with limited atonement.

First of all, we remember what the Bible teaches about election. Before the foundation of the world, God chose to save some sinners. "Those whom he foreknew he also predestined to be conformed to the image of his Son" (Rom. 8:29). Paul also said that the Father chose his people in Christ (Eph. 1:4). This means that God chose his people and sent his Son to save them from their sins. When Jesus prayed to the Father, he prayed for the people whom God had given him (John 17:2, 6–9). Like the high priest entered into God's presence on behalf of the Israelites, so Jesus entered into God's presence on behalf of the elect (Heb. 9). God's will is that Christ keeps and saves all that he has given him (John 6:39). Jesus died to save the elect.

The second thing to think about is how the Bible describes the outcome of Jesus' death. Matthew tells us that his name is Jesus because "he will save his people from their sins" (Matt. 1:21). Jesus knows his sheep and he laid down his life for them

(Ezek. 34:11–12; John 10:14–15). He gave up his life for the church (Eph. 5:25–26). In his death Jesus accomplished his mission of saving *his* people, not all people.

Very often Paul uses the term *for us* when he talks about Christ's death. Paul wrote his letters to Christians, so *for us* means *for Christians*. "While we were still sinners, Christ died for us" (Rom. 5:8). He "redeemed us from the curse of the law by becoming a curse for us" (Gal. 3:13). Christ "loved us and gave himself up for us" (Eph. 5:2). Jesus "gave himself for us to redeem us from all lawlessness" (Titus 2:14). The apostle John wrote that Jesus loved his people so much that "he laid down his life for us" (1 John 3:16). Again, we see that Jesus didn't die to make redemption possible for everyone. He died to actually redeem and save his people.

➦ Jesus gave up his life for his church.

OTHER THINGS . . .

There are some other things we should think about. If Christ did die for everyone, in some ways he was a failure, because some people are in hell. This makes Jesus seem weak, because many people he died for do not go to heaven. But the Bible teaches Jesus died to *save* his people. None of his people will be lost (John 10:28–29).

One Arminian Christian once said that Jesus' death makes all people savable (able to be saved). Again, this makes Jesus look weak because it means he didn't actually save people by his death. Think of the lifeguard again. The lifeguard who only throws a rope to drowning people isn't a good lifeguard.

The lifeguard whom we'd want to have is the one who jumps in, grabs drowning people, and brings them safely to shore. That's what Jesus did. He really and truly rescued the elect when he died and rose again.

ALL . . . ?

There are a few verses in the Bible that seem to teach that Jesus died for everyone. For example, Paul said that Jesus "gave himself as a ransom for all" (1 Tim. 2:6; see also John 1:29; 3:16; 2 Cor. 5:14–15; 1 John 2:2). We don't have the space here to talk about all these verses. But we should think about them, of course, since they're in the Bible.

When we think about these verses, we can't forget the other Bible teachings we learned. The Bible teaches that God chose to save some people and pass by others (unconditional election). The Bible teaches that Jesus' death actually redeemed his people (definite atonement). It is also important to know that the Bible uses the word *all* like we do. Sometimes when we say *all* we mean *every single one*. But sometimes when we say *all* we mean *many* or *all kinds*. Let's say you're sitting in a stadium watching a baseball game. While you're there, a man says, "All the people are wearing red." First of all, he's not talking about people outside the stadium. Second, even if there were a few people in the stadium wearing blue, the statement is still correct. The word *all* means *many* or *all kinds of people*. This is just how we use language. The Bible uses it this way too.

➡ The Bible uses the word *all* like we do.

If you read Acts 9:32–35, you'll see that it says *all* the people of two cities believed in the Lord. This means that *many* or *all kinds of people* believed. Sometimes in the Bible *world* also means *many* or *all kinds of people*. For example, one time when many people were following Jesus, the Pharisees said, "Look, the world has gone after him" (John 12:19). In other words, all kinds of people followed Jesus.

So when we read verses in the Bible that say Jesus died for *all* or *the world*, remember these things: (1) what election means, (2) what the atonement means, and (3) how the words *all* and *world* are used in the Bible. Keeping these three things in mind, we can still say that Jesus died for his people, the elect. When the Bible says that Jesus died for *all* or for *the world*, it means that Jesus died for all kinds of people from all around the world. When we tell others about Jesus, the free offer of the gospel is that whoever truly believes will be truly saved. We don't know who are elect, but we know that whoever believes will be saved.

SUMMARY . . .

Limited atonement means Jesus definitely saved his people when he died. His death means definite salvation for God's elect. This is good news! Jesus didn't leave his saving work unfinished. In fact, he said, "It is finished" (John 19:28, 30)! When we tell others about Jesus, we can say for sure that he has accomplished salvation for all who believe in him. He has done it all.

STUDY QUESTIONS

1. Explain the lifeguard story in this lesson.
2. Which lifeguard would you want? Explain how this compares to Jesus as our Savior.

3. How are election and limited atonement related?

4. Explain what we learned about the phrase *for us* in this lesson.

5. Do you think it is okay for Christians to be certain that Christ died for them and that they will for sure go to heaven? Explain.

6. We've been using the terms *definite* and *limited* to define Christ's atonement. Which do you think is better, and why?

7. In the Bible, do the words *all* and *the world* always mean every person? Explain.

8. List some verses about limited atonement that you find helpful.

9. In a short paragraph, explain limited atonement in your own words.

10. What comfort can we receive from the last words of this lesson (Jesus has done it all)?

MEMORY WORK

I am the good shepherd. I know my own and my own know me . . . and I lay down my life for the sheep. (John 10:14–15)

[Jesus prayed] I am praying for them. I am not praying for the world but for those whom you have given me, for they are yours. (John 17:9)

SAVING THE DEAD

This lesson, like every other one in this book, is about God's grace in saving sinners. We have studied a lot of different things so far—things like total depravity, unconditional election, and limited atonement. But we don't want to treat these truths like boring statements. We are learning about *salvation from sin!* We should pray that these truths of salvation give us joy, happiness, and hope in life and in death.

➲ We are learning about salvation from sin!

This lesson on irresistible grace (the *I* in TULIP) is very personal. In other words, it is all about a person becoming a Christian. We're going to learn how the Holy Spirit changes a totally depraved sinner into a believing Christian. The Canons of Dort call this change "most delightful, astonishing, [and] mysterious" (III/IV, article 12).

A CHRISTIAN . . .

How does a person who is not a Christian actually become a Christian? Some people say that you can become a Christian sort of like you become a member of a club. All you have to do is decide one day to join the club. That's what some people say about Christianity.

Other people say that God wants people to be Christians and Satan doesn't want people to be Christians. People are the ones who make the final choice. In other words, it's up to a person to become a Christian. God might help them a little, but mostly it's up to them.

But we already learned that the Bible says all people are born in sin. They are also totally depraved. Sin has messed up every part of all people. We also learned that people are stuck in sin. They are in bondage to sin and can't just stop sinning whenever they want. Sinners can't choose to believe in Jesus because they are trapped in sin.

How can someone become a Christian? It is possible, of course! According to the doctrines of grace, the only way someone can become a Christian is if *God* changes his heart and mind. Since we can't turn ourselves toward God, he turns us toward himself. We cannot say that people turn to God using their free will. Instead, we say this turning is something God alone does (Canons III/IV, article 10). John Calvin said this turning is "entirely and without exception from God."[1]

REGENERATION . . .

We're learning a lot of words in these lessons. Another one is *regeneration*. Regeneration is the word we use to describe when a person's heart is changed and he believes in Jesus. The Bible calls it being "born again" through the living word of God (John

1. John Calvin, *Institutes of the Christian Religion* (Louisville: Westminster John Knox, 1960), III.XV.7.

3:3; 1 Peter 1:3, 23). It is also called "new life" (Rom. 6:4; 7:6). The prophet Ezekiel described regeneration as God giving his people a "new heart." God said he will "remove the heart of stone" and give his people a "heart of flesh" (Ezek. 36:26). This is regeneration.

A person who doesn't believe in Jesus is spiritually dead. He or she has a hard and cold heart that doesn't believe in the true God. So when God changes dead and cold hearts, he gives them new life and faith in Christ. An older English word for this is *quickening*. Paul said it this way: "If anyone is in Christ, he is a new creation. The old has passed away; behold, the new has come. All this is from God" (2 Cor. 5:17–18). By Christ's power we are "raised up to a new life" (Heidelberg Catechism, Q/A 45).

⮞ By Christ's power we are "raised up to a new life."

NEW LIFE . . .

One of the clearest places in the Bible that talks about God giving new life to a sinner is Ephesians 2:4–5:

> But God, being rich in mercy, because of the great love with which he loved us, even when we were dead in our trespasses, made us alive together with Christ—by grace you have been saved.

Paul wrote this very clearly. We were dead in sin, but because he loved us, God gave us new life in Christ. A Christian can truly say, "I once was dead in sin, but God gave me a new heart and new life. Now I am alive!"

A few lessons ago we heard a story about a seminary professor and a graveyard. He told his students to preach to the dead bodies in the ground. The students of course could not make the dead bodies get up. Only God could do that. This is what happens when God changes the heart and mind of a person who is dead in sin. He gives spiritual life where there was only death and darkness before. God "saved us . . . by the washing of regeneration and renewal of the Holy Spirit" (Titus 3:5).

Think about it. A dead person cannot get up. He cannot take medicine that a doctor is trying to give him. He is dead. So it is with a sinner. Only God can give new life to people who are dead in sin. He gives them the life-giving medicine of the gospel. And when he does this, they believe in Christ and enjoy new life as a child of God.

⮞   A dead person cannot get up.

IRRESISTIBLE GRACE . . .

If you've been paying attention, you may have noticed we didn't yet define the *I* in TULIP. *I* stands for irresistible grace. This means that God sovereignly gives life to a dead heart. "The Spirit gives life" (2 Cor. 3:6; John 6:63). Sinners cannot resist God for two reasons. First, they are dead in sin. Second, God's will is more powerful than their will. Just like in election and the atonement, God is the one who is in control of saving sinners. He gives life to dead hearts.

The word *irresistible* may sound like God forces people to be Christians even if they don't want to. But it just means that God's grace is stronger than a person's sinful and dead heart. A better way to say it is that God's grace is invincible or effective. God effectively changes a dead person's heart and gives him or her faith. When he does that, people *want* to be called Christians. They then love Jesus and believe in him. The Westminster Larger Catechism names this "effectual calling" (Q/A 67).

⮑ God's grace is invincible.

Arminians say that God gives everyone grace and they can decide whether to believe in Jesus or not. But we've already learned that this is wrong. No one can just decide to believe when he or she wants, because all are in bondage to sin. A person dead in sin doesn't even *want to* believe! If a person is going to become a Christian, God must work a miracle. He must change a dead heart and give it life. When he does that, a person believes in Jesus and becomes a Christian. With his or her new heart the person loves the Lord and his Word.

SUMMARY . . .

Since all people are dead in sin, they cannot turn to Christ. However, in his power and grace, the Holy Spirit changes dead hearts. This is called regeneration, new birth, and new life. The *I* in TULIP means irresistible grace. God's grace effectively changes people and makes them believers. They are Christians because the Father chose them, the Son died for them, and the Holy Spirit changed their hearts.

When we study these doctrines, we just can't get away from grace! God's grace doesn't mean he wants people to believe and he hopes they some day believe. God's grace means he seeks his people, finds them, and gives them new life. Peter knew it when he said this: "Blessed be the God and Father of our Lord Jesus Christ! According to his great mercy, he has caused us to be born again to a living hope through the resurrection of Jesus Christ from the dead" (1 Peter 1:3).

STUDY QUESTIONS

1. What do some people say about becoming a Christian?
2. What does the Bible say about becoming a Christian?
3. What is regeneration?
4. Write out Ezekiel 36:26.
5. What is one of the clearest places in the Bible that talks about regeneration? What does it say about regeneration?
6. What does *irresistible grace* mean?
7. What do Arminians teach about grace?
8. Based on this lesson, would you say that a person believes in Jesus after regeneration or before? Explain.
9. Is the teaching of irresistible grace part of the good news (the gospel)? If so, how?
10. How does it bring us hope to know that God's grace can change any hard heart?
11. What does this mean for you when you deal with part of your heart that might still be hard?

MEMORY WORK

He saved us . . . by the washing of regeneration and renewal of the Holy Spirit. (Titus 3:5)

According to his great mercy, he has caused us to be born again to a living hope through the resurrection of Jesus Christ from the dead. (1 Peter 1:3)

POWERFUL WORDS

We can do a quick review of our last lesson by mentioning Ezekiel 37. In Ezekiel 37 there's an amazing story where God tells Ezekiel to preach over a whole bunch of dead bones. He does, and they stand up and live. Then God tells Ezekiel that he is the Lord who gives life to his people by the power of his Holy Spirit. Another story like this is the story of Jesus raising Lazarus from the dead (John 11).

Regeneration is like those Bible stories. God lovingly and powerfully gives life to his people who are dead in sin. That's how a sinner becomes a Christian. The Westminster Confession says that God effectively draws his elect to himself (10.1). This is irresistible grace.

CALLING . . .

The Bible does tell us more about regeneration and irresistible grace. It also talks about God calling his people. For example, remember when Jesus called his disciples? He said, "Follow me, and I will make you fishers of men"

(Matt. 4:19). What happened? "Immediately they left their nets and followed him" (Matt. 4:20). Jesus' call was effective. His words were powerful enough to make regular people drop what they were doing and follow him. His words made them disciples.

◆ Jesus' words are powerful.

Jesus also said it this way: "No one can come to me unless the Father who sent me draws him" (John 6:44). Jesus speaks to his people, the Father draws them in, and the Spirit changes their hearts. The triune God brings his people to himself and gives them faith. He effectually calls dead sinners, gives them life, and makes them Christians.

When we studied election we learned that Jesus died for his sheep because he loves them (John 10:15). The Bible also says that Jesus' sheep hear his voice and follow him (John 10:27). Jesus has the "words of eternal life" (John 6:68). He speaks loving words to his sheep all around the world and they come to him (John 10:14–16). When Jesus calls, his people come.

WORDS . . .

When we talk about God calling sinners to himself, we notice that he uses words. God usually doesn't just zap a person on the sidewalk and change his or her heart out of the blue. Just like Jesus used words to call his disciples, he also uses words to call people today. People don't become Christians by staring at the sky. Sinners' hearts aren't changed when they play soccer. People become Christians when they truly hear Jesus' words. Their hearts are changed when Jesus calls them. Paul knew this pretty well since Jesus called him out of darkness.

How does Jesus call his people? He speaks his word to them. Paul said that "faith comes from hearing, and hearing through the word of Christ" (Rom. 10:17). We learn more about this in the New Testament book of Acts. Acts tells the story of the early Christian church. The church grew by the preaching of the Word. One thing the early church always did was preach sermons about Jesus the Messiah who died, rose again, and ascended into heaven (Acts 5:42). He added to his church through the preaching of the gospel (Acts 2:42–47; 11:24).

⮕ The church grew by the preaching of the Word.

Since Jesus is in heaven, he uses his people to call others. Jesus told his apostles they would be his witnesses to the ends of the earth (Acts 1:8). Although there are no more apostles, Jesus sends preachers and missionaries to bring his word of salvation to his people all over the world (Rom. 10:14–15). Christian churches today still pray that God would send his good news to people in all different countries.

IMPORTANT . . .

This is why we say preaching is so important. Some people think preaching is boring. Others think preaching doesn't work. But the Bible says preaching is very important (2 Tim. 4:1–3).

And it works! By the power of his Holy Spirit, Jesus uses his preached Word to change dead hearts. He sends his Word and Spirit to give life to his people. God said, "My word . . . shall accomplish that which I purpose, and shall succeed in the thing for which I sent it" (Isa. 55:11).

We can be very thankful that Jesus' Word is strong enough to change dead hearts and closed minds. If Jesus' words weren't powerful, everyone would be lost forever! It's not like Jesus calls people and hopes that they respond. They can't, because they're unable. No one can get up and follow, because all people are dead in sin! So when Jesus speaks, he gives life to dead hearts by the power of his Word and Spirit.

COME . . .

We do have to go to Christ. We do have to believe in Jesus. We have to repent of our sins. Our parents or friends can't repent and believe for us. No one can be saved if he or she does not repent and believe in Jesus. Don't finish these lessons and think you don't have to repent of your sins and believe in Jesus! "Repent and believe in the gospel" (Mark 1:15)!

➡ Our parents or friends can't repent and believe for us.

A Christian is someone who turns away from sin to Jesus. But we know that God is the one who changes the hearts of his people. Because he changes hearts, Christians understand that the triune God deserves all the credit for giving us new life, repentance, and faith.

The story of Lydia in Acts is a good one to think about here. Lydia was a regular woman in a Greek city called Philippi. One day Paul preached there. She heard about Jesus and believed in him. Acts 16:14 says, "The Lord opened her heart to respond to Paul's message" (NIV). In other words, she did believe, but only because God was working in her. He opened her heart, and she believed in Jesus.

There are other ways the Bible describes this. For example, Isaiah said, "The Sovereign LORD has opened my ears" (Isa. 50:5 NIV). Jesus also opens peoples' minds so they understand the Scriptures (Luke 24:32). God causes his people to repent (Acts 11:18). The Lord gives his people understanding so they may know him who is true (1 John 5:20). They love him because he loved them first (1 John 4:19).

We do have to repent and believe. But when we do, we thank God that he gave us a new heart. He chased after us, found us, and changed our hearts. Because he did this we believe in him, love him, and follow him. We do come to him, but only because he came to us first.

SUMMARY . . .

Irresistible grace is all about God's mercy and love to sinners. He not only chose to save some sinners, he also sent his Son to die for them. But he didn't stop there. He also effectively calls his elect to himself. He changes dead hearts and gives them life by his Word and Spirit. The doctrines of grace are all connected because God's plan to save sinners is perfect. "Those whom he predestined he also called, and those whom he called he also justified, and those whom he justified he also glorified" (Rom. 8:30).

God's grace in changing dead hearts and giving them life is good for us to remember when we tell others about Jesus. It's not up to us to change hearts. And no matter how sinful a person is, God is powerful enough to change *any* heart. Because of this fact, we can be certain that missions and evangelism will result in changed hearts and lives.

> ⮑ It's not up to us to change hearts.

STUDY QUESTIONS

1. Review: what does regeneration mean?
2. What two Bible stories are good examples of regeneration?
3. Explain Jesus' effective call in Matthew 4:19–20.
4. Explain the meaning of irresistible grace using the biblical pictures of Jesus as a shepherd with sheep.
5. Does God usually "zap" people and make them Christians? How does he usually work?
6. If someone told you that churches should forget about preaching because nobody likes it, what would you say?
7. Is it possible to be a Christian without repenting of sin and believing in Jesus? Explain.
8. When a person does repent and believe, who deserves the credit? What does this mean in your own prayers?
9. In four or more sentences, explain irresistible grace.
10. What does this teaching mean for you when you tell an unbeliever about Jesus? Do you have to stress out if you didn't present the gospel perfectly?

11. How would you encourage your pastor, a missionary, or a church planter based on this teaching of irresistible grace?

MEMORY WORK

My word . . . shall accomplish that which I purpose, and shall succeed in the thing for which I sent it. (Isa. 55:11)

Those whom he predestined he also called, and those whom he called he also justified, and those whom he justified he also glorified. (Rom. 8:30)

CHAPTER

10

WHO'S A SAINT?

We're almost done with our short study of the doctrines of grace (TULIP). We'll do a full review
after we talk about the *P* of TULIP. *P* stands for
perseverance of the saints. For many Christians this biblical
teaching is very comforting. Since we still struggle with sin,
it is a great thing to know Jesus will hold on to us no matter
what happens.

We've been seeing that all these doctrines of grace are
very practical. They matter for us in our everyday lives. These
truths of salvation give us comfort and joy when we're healthy,
when we're sick, and even when we face death. The Heidelberg
Catechism is right: our only comfort in life and in death is that
we belong to our faithful Savior, Jesus Christ (Q/A 1).

SAINTS . . .

We're going to learn about the word *saints* before we learn
about perseverance. Sometimes when we hear the word *saint* we
think of a person who is almost perfect. But a better meaning
for this word is "set apart." A saint is someone who has been

called by God and set apart from the world (Ps. 37:28). Those who are loved by God are "called to be saints" (Rom. 1:7).

Of course someone who believes in Christ does his or her best to obey Jesus. In one sense a Christian is a saint because he or she doesn't do all the wicked things that many unbelievers do (Eph. 5:3). But Christians are called saints mostly because the Father elected them, Jesus died for them, and the Holy Spirit gave them new life. These are the doctrines we talked about in earlier lessons.

Who is a saint? A saint is a true Christian! The Bible says that everyone who calls on the Lord Jesus Christ is a saint (1 Cor. 1:2). A saint isn't someone who just *says* he or she believes in Jesus. A saint is a real Christian who truly loves the Lord. Saints are people who repent of their sin and fight against it. A saint isn't a perfect person, but someone whose sins have been washed away by Christ's blood. You are a saint if you are a real Christian.

➲   A saint is a true Christian.

PERSEVERANCE . . .

The next word we need to learn is *perseverance*. To persevere means to make it to the end. If a woman runs a marathon, she's going to need perseverance to finish. If she does finish, we say she persevered.

In the Bible perseverance means almost the same thing. For example, Hebrews 12:1 says this: "Let us run with perseverance the race marked out for us" (NIV). In this part of Hebrews, we are called to keep our eyes focused on Jesus.

Even when life gets tough, or when people make fun of us for being a Christian, we have to keep running this race. We can't give up. We need to persevere. The Canons of Dort say that perseverance includes pressing forward to the goal of perfection (V, article 2).

James also talked about perseverance. "Blessed is the man who perseveres under trial, because when he has stood the test, he will receive the crown of life that God has promised to those who love him" (James 1:12 NIV). In the Christian life, perseverance means following Jesus no matter what happens. The Bible calls Christians to stay strong in the faith and not turn away from Jesus (1 Cor. 9:24–27; 15:58; Gal. 6:9; 1 Thess. 2:12; 2 Peter 1:10; etc.).

It isn't an odd thing that the Bible calls Christians to be strong in the faith. Barnabas encouraged new Christians to "remain true to the Lord with all their hearts" (Acts 11:23 NIV). Even though we do believe in Jesus, sometimes we wander off the Christian path. Sometimes we get lazy in the faith. Sometimes being a Christian is very hard and we think about giving up. So God's Word encourages us to stay on the path. It is a lamp to our feet and a light to our path (Ps. 119:105). The Bible reminds us that God is with us and that a great future in heaven awaits us. We need encouragement to stand firm and follow our Lord Jesus.

⮞ God's Word encourages us to stay on the path.

DOCTRINE . . .

The Bible also teaches that God will keep his people. We've already talked about Jesus dying to save his sheep. We also learned that Jesus' sheep hear his voice. But Jesus didn't just die for his sheep and call them to himself. He also keeps them. "I give them eternal life, and they will never perish, and no one will snatch them out of my hand. . . . No one is able to snatch them out of the Father's hand" (John 10:28–29).

Jesus is the Good Shepherd. He loves his sheep so much that he died for them, calls them into his flock, and keeps them in his flock forever. Of course sometimes the sheep are disobedient. But he doesn't hate them and let the wolves eat them. He uses his staff to lovingly bring wandering sheep back into the pen. Jesus will not let them go, because they are his.

PRESERVATION . . .

Maybe we should say the *P* in TULIP means the preservation of the saints. This means that *God* preserves the saints. He keeps them forever. Psalm 37:28 says this clearly: "The Lord . . . will not forsake his saints. They are preserved forever." Psalm 97:10 says the same thing: "The Lord . . . preserves the lives of his saints." With his strong and loving arms, Jesus holds tightly to his people.

If God would let us walk the path of Christianity on our own strength, we would probably give up in just a few weeks. Because he loves us, God doesn't just change our hearts and let us go. He continues to work in us by the power of his Holy Spirit. "He who began a good work in you will bring it to completion" (Phil. 1:6). Paul knew Jesus would bring him safely into the heavenly kingdom (2 Tim. 4:18). In the words of the Canons of Dort, God "powerfully preserves" his people in saving grace to the end (V, article 3).

We shouldn't grow lazy in the Christian faith. We shouldn't forget what the Bible teaches about salvation from sin. We shouldn't live sinful lives like unbelievers. We need to follow Christ in faith and obedience. But we don't depend on our own strength to make it. We depend on the power of Christ, which is at work within us (Eph. 3:20).

The Christian will make it to the end because he can do all things through *Christ* who gives him strength (Phil. 4:13). In A.D. 429 Augustine wrote a book about this called *A Treatise on the Gift of Perseverance*. His words are helpful: "The perseverance by which we persevere in Christ to the end is the gift of God." In other words, we're saved by grace and kept by grace.

➠ We're saved by grace and kept by grace.

SUMMARY . . .

This doctrine of grace, the perseverance of the saints, means that God will keep his people to the end. Jesus will certainly bring true Christians to heaven. He is stronger than Satan, sin, and hell. Therefore nothing will separate Christians from Christ (Rom. 8:35–39). Jesus died for his people, and he will not let them go. His love is strong!

This is one reason we sing praises to God. In his steadfast love and faithfulness he preserves his people (Ps. 40:11). Even though we still sin, Jesus holds on to us in love. This should cause us to say the words of Psalm 34:1: "I will bless the LORD at all times; his praise shall continually be in my mouth."

STUDY QUESTIONS

1. Is a saint someone who is almost perfect? What then?
2. What does *perseverance* mean?
3. Do you think it is strange that the Bible encourages Christians to follow Jesus even when life is tough? Explain.
4. When we speak about Jesus as the Shepherd of his sheep, what does it have to do with election, Christ's death, and perseverance?
5. What else can the *P* in TULIP stand for?
6. What would happen if a Christian had to depend on his own strength to follow Jesus?
7. Should we do our best to obey Christ and live godly lives? Why?
8. What do we depend on to persevere?
9. What does perseverance of the saints mean for Christians who might get discouraged because their growth and obedience seem so weak?
10. How is this teaching a comfort to you when you stumble in sin?

MEMORY WORK

The LORD . . . will not forsake his saints. They are preserved forever. (Ps. 37:28)

For I am sure that neither death nor life, nor angels nor rulers, nor things present nor things to come, nor powers, nor height nor depth, nor anything else in all creation, will be able to separate us from the love of God in Christ Jesus our Lord. (Rom. 8:38–39)

FROM START TO FINISH

In our last lesson we learned that the *P* in TULIP means the perseverance of the saints. It also means the preservation of the saints. That is, God preserves true Christians. Don't forget Psalm 37:28: "The LORD . . . will not forsake his saints. They are preserved forever." No one can snatch Jesus' sheep out of his hand (John 10:28–29).

The Westminster Confession says that those whom God has effectually called will never totally fall away from him. They "shall certainly persevere . . . to the end, and be eternally saved" (17.1). Arminians and Roman Catholics believe that a true Christian can fall away and not end up in heaven. But Reformed Christians disagree. We believe the elect will persevere by God's grace. God will finish his work of salvation.

⮕ God will finish his work of salvation.

SCRIPTURE . . .

In this lesson, we're going to study some more Bible verses that talk about this doctrine of grace. Just like the other doctrines of grace, we want to be sure we do our best to follow the Bible's teaching.

First of all, God's love for his people is eternal. He tells his people, "My steadfast love shall not depart from you, and my covenant of peace shall not be removed" (Isa. 54:10). The Lord's covenant love for his people means he will not turn away from them. It also means his people will not turn away from him (Jer. 32:40). There's an unbreakable bond of love between God and his people (Rom. 8:38–39). He will preserve them.

This love has to do with eternal life. Whoever truly believes in Jesus will not "perish but have eternal life" (John 3:16). Jesus gives his sheep eternal life (John 10:28). He will not cast away anyone who comes to him (John 6:35–40). Jesus *will* raise his people from the dead when he returns (John 6:40). The Good Shepherd will lead his sheep all the days of their lives. They will "dwell in the house of the LORD forever" (Ps. 23:6).

THINK ABOUT . . .

If God truly forgives a person, he will never take away his forgiveness (Isa. 43:25). If God truly justifies a person, he will not unjustify or condemn the person (Rom. 8:33–34). If God truly adopts a person into his family, he will not cancel the adoption (Eph. 1:5). If God is truly sanctifying someone, he will not just stop doing it (Phil. 1:6). If God chose a person, washed the person in Christ's blood, changed the person's heart, and gave him or her new life, this person will be glorified (Rom. 8:30).

Sometimes we start a project and don't finish it. We start to write a letter but give up. Or we think about going for a jog but don't do it because we're too tired. God is not like us in this way. He doesn't give up or quit doing his work. He doesn't stop being a Good Shepherd. One pastor said it well: "God always finishes what he starts, especially the salvation of his people." The Christian can really say, "The LORD will fulfill his purpose for me" (Ps. 138:8).

◆⟩ God always finishes what he starts.

You might know people who used to go to church but now they don't. It seems like they just quit being Christians. But people who never come back to the church weren't true Christians in the first place. This happened in the early church. John explained it like this: "They went out from us, but they did not really belong to us. For if they had belonged to us, they would have remained with us; but their going showed that none of them belonged to us" (1 John 2:19 NIV). Jesus said this was like a seed that grows for a little while but eventually dies because its roots aren't deep (Matt. 13:20–21).

THE CORINTHIANS . . .

The Corinthian Christians were involved in some terrible sins (R-rated sins!). But Paul knew that God would not forsake them, because Jesus died for them. He even called them *saints* (1 Cor. 1:1–2)! Paul told them that because God is faithful, he would not let them be tempted beyond their strength. Paul said that God would provide a way of escape so they would endure (1 Cor. 10:13). A true Christian can fall *down* in the faith, but not *away*.

79

Paul did rebuke the Corinthians for their sin, because they were wandering from the path. He told them to stop disobeying God. Paul said they should live like saints, not sinners. He also reminded them about their salvation in Christ (1 Cor. 15). Just like God raised Jesus from the dead, so he would raise them from the dead as well (1 Cor. 6:14). Paul told them that the "Lord Jesus Christ . . . will sustain you to the end" (1 Cor. 1:7–8).

Peter's story is like the story of the Corinthian church. He sinned terribly by doubting Jesus and telling him the cross was a bad idea. Peter even denied Jesus three times! Jesus could have let Peter go. But he didn't. Instead, he kept Peter: "I have prayed for you [Peter] that your faith may not fail" (Luke 22:32). Jesus' prayer was powerful. Peter's faith did not fail. In fact, he went on to write two letters to the early church! Peter is with Jesus in heaven now (2 Peter 1:14).

RELATED . . .

The *P* in TULIP is related to the other letters. All the doctrines of grace go hand in hand. Here's how it works:

- *T* and *I*: Those whom the Spirit gave new life will not go back to being dead in sin (2 Cor. 1:22; 5:5).
- *U*: Those whom the Father elects he elects to salvation. He will not unelect someone he's chosen by grace (Rom. 9:11).
- *L*: Those whom Christ died for are promised eternal life. His saving work on the cross cannot be undone (John 10:28).
- *P*: God will finish the work of salvation he's started in his people (Phil. 1:6).

➜ The doctrines of grace are all related.

In his sovereignty our triune God saves his people from start to finish. Just like he powerfully upholds the whole creation, he also powerfully upholds his people. Providence and perseverance go together.

We persevere not because of our love or strength, but because of God's loving strength. While we should hate the sin in us, we should not lose hope because of it. Also, we should obey Jesus and follow him. But we depend on Jesus, not on our works, to bring us to heaven. "We persevere because we are preserved by God."[1]

SUMMARY . . .

God's elect persevere in the Christian faith because God preserves them in it. People who are truly saints will be with the Lord in the new creation (Isa. 65:17–19). Real Christians will certainly go to heaven, because God will bring them there. God's promises will not fail (Canons V, article 8). This is the *P* in TULIP.

Some people say that this teaching makes Christians lazy in the faith. But it shouldn't! If a Christian really understands he deserves to go to hell but God saved him from it, he won't be lazy. He will instead be very thankful. He will want to praise the Lord no matter what. If this teaching makes people lazy, they don't really get it!

It is true that we would fall away from Jesus if we had to depend on our own strength. But because God is faithful and

1. R. C. Sproul, *Grace Unknown* (Grand Rapids: Baker, 1997), 197.

loving, and because he keeps his promises, we can be sure he will keep us in the faith. Because Jesus' work on the cross saved us, because the Spirit is at work within us, nothing will separate us from the Lord. Yes, we should hate sin and follow Jesus in obedience, but we should do so depending on him to hold onto us. Jesus loves his own people "to the end" (John 13:1).

STUDY QUESTIONS

1. What does the Westminster Confession of Faith say about perseverance of the saints?
2. Explain what God's love has to do with the *P* in TULIP.
3. Will God unadopt his children? Read Ephesians 1:5–7 and explain.
4. Describe the situation in Corinth and relate it to perseverance.
5. How do the *U* and the *P* go together in TULIP?
6. How do the *L* and the *P* go together in TULIP?
7. Describe how the lesson put providence and perseverance together.
8. True or false: since Jesus will certainly keep his people, that means we can go on sinning and do anything we want. Explain your answer.
9. What would you say to someone who says he or she is a Christian but doesn't care about obeying Jesus?
10. What does it mean for you, and other true Christians, that *nothing* can separate you from the love of God in Christ?
11. What does the perseverance of the saints mean for you when you face tough times in life (for example, when

you face the death of a family member, terrible sickness, or depression)?

MEMORY WORK

He who began a good work in you will bring it to completion at the day of Jesus Christ. (Phil. 1:6)

The Lord will rescue me from every evil deed and bring me safely into his heavenly kingdom. (2 Tim. 4:18)

A REVIEW

God's grace is truly amazing. There is nothing more amazing anywhere! Since all people are terribly sinful, God didn't have to save anyone. But because he is a God of love and mercy, he chose to save some sinners. He didn't just make salvation possible. The Father actually redeemed his people by giving his Son to die and his Spirit to give life to dead hearts. In all of this, he is glorified as the gracious Savior and Redeemer. From start to finish, salvation belongs to the Lord! This is the main story of the Bible.

TULIP . . .

If you've studied this book, you should now know the basics of the doctrines of grace. You should know what TULIP stands for. We'll do a quick review here so you don't forget. And remember, the Arminian five points are opposite of these.

T stands for *total depravity.* We learned about this in lessons 2 and 3. There we studied Bible verses that talk about sin. All people are conceived and born in sin. All people are in bondage to sin and do not have free will to choose Jesus on their own. Though people aren't as sinful as they could possibly be, every part of a person is messed up by sin.

U stands for *unconditional election*. We learned about this in lessons 4 and 5. It means that God elected his people before he created the world. He chose people not because they believed. He chose people who were dead in sin. Election is not conditional on faith. Election is based on God's choice, not ours.

L stands for *limited atonement*. We learned about this in lessons 6 and 7. The Bible teaches that Jesus died for his sheep. He died to save the church. He atoned for the sins of the elect. He didn't come to make salvation a possibility. He came to definitely save his people. We can also call this *definite atonement*.

I stands for *irresistible grace*. We learned about this in lessons 8 and 9. The Bible teaches that the Holy Spirit effectively calls and regenerates the elect. He changes their dead hearts and gives them faith in Jesus. Jesus' sheep hear his voice and come to him. Another way to say this is effective or invincible grace.

P stands for *perseverance of the saints*. We learned about this in lessons 10 and 11. The Bible teaches that God will never forsake his elect. Jesus will not cast his sheep away. The Lord will complete the work he's begun in his people. Nothing can separate us from his love. Perseverance means that God preserves his people to the end.

REFORMED . . .

These doctrines of grace are part of Reformed (and Presbyterian) theology. They are found in the Westminster Standards and the Three Forms of Unity. The Canons of Dort specifically explain the doctrines of grace (the order is ULTIP). The Reformers taught these truths because they found them in the Bible. They disagreed with Roman Catholic doctrine and with Arminian teaching. If people don't believe in these doctrines of grace, they cannot call themselves Reformed.

⮞ TULIP is part of Reformed theology.

Of course there's a lot more to Reformed theology than TULIP. Reformed Christians also believe that our triune God, before the foundation of the world, sovereignly decreed how history would unfold—with Christ and his people at the center. We also believe that God's covenant of grace includes parents and their children, which is why we baptize children. Reformed Christians believe churches are connected to each other, so we have church meetings called general assemblies or synods. Reformed Christians also believe that we should worship God only as he told us to do in his Word. Reformed theology also teaches other biblical truths. TULIP is only part of what it means to be Reformed.

⮞ There's a lot more to Reformed theology than TULIP.

We also believe that Christians who do not believe TULIP are still Christians. Even though John Calvin and Martin Luther had some different beliefs, they didn't hate each other, because they agreed on the main teachings of the Bible. While we believe Arminian teaching isn't as biblical as it could be, we consider them Christians because many of them confess the main truths of Christianity with us. Together with us, for example, they believe the Apostles' Creed is a good summary of the Christian faith.

CHRISTIAN LIVING . . .

In these lessons, we've learned that the doctrines of grace aren't like mathematics. It's not like we say 2 + 2 = 4 is true and then forget about it. These doctrines are not just for our heads but for our hearts as well. The more we learn about grace, the more our lives should change. The more we learn about how God has saved us from sin, the more we learn to praise and thank him all the time.

➔ TULIP is for our heads and hearts.

The way Paul wrote the book of Romans has everything to do with the Christian life. First he talks about sin and guilt (1:18–3:20). Then he talks about how God graciously saves his people from sin and guilt (3:21–11:36). Finally, Paul tells Christians that we should live lives of service to show God gratitude for saving us from sin (12:1–16:27). This is how the Heidelberg Catechism was written as well: sin, salvation, and service; or guilt, grace, and gratitude. This is a biblical way to talk about the Christian life.

It is sad to say that some Christians who believe the doctrines of grace (TULIP) don't live godly lives. Some people who believe in the doctrines of grace are cocky. They think that they are better because they know true doctrine. But these people are not living like good Calvinists. They are being inconsistent. A consistent Calvinist will not think he or she is better than other people. Consistent Calvinists will know that they deserved to be punished in hell forever but God saved them by grace alone. They will not pray like the Pharisee ("God, I thank you that I am not [sinful] like other men"). They will always pray like the tax collector ("God, be merciful to me, a sinner!") (Luke 18:11–14).

➡ God, be merciful to me, a sinner!

Christians who truly understand the doctrines of grace will love other people, even our enemies. We will want to tell others about Jesus because we know he is a real and powerful Savior. He can change the hardest heart in the world through our words (even if we make some mistakes!). If we've been saved by God's grace, we will want others to have the same joy we do. Those who believe in the doctrines of grace should be very involved in missions and evangelism.

CONCLUSION . . .

These doctrines of grace should lead us to grow in godliness. As we learn more and more about God's grace, we should more and more want to live obedient lives to glorify him. We know that he loved us first, but we do love him in return (1 John 4:19). Reformed Christians should hate sin, fight it with all their might, and pray that God would make them more like Christ each day.

Let me encourage you as we end these lessons. Hide God's Word in your heart so that you can better fight sin (Ps. 119:11). Go to church often where you can hear about Jesus saving sinners. This is how God makes us better Christians (Acts 20:32). Pray that the Lord would help you understand his grace more and help you obey him (Ps. 119:34). And never lose hope, because Jesus will keep his people no matter what.

STUDY QUESTIONS

1. What does *T* stand for? Explain it with a few sentences.
2. What does *U* stand for? Explain it with a few sentences.
3. What does *L* stand for? Explain it with a few sentences.
4. What does *I* stand for? Explain it with a few sentences.
5. What does *P* stand for? Explain it with a few sentences.
6. Is there more to Reformed theology than TULIP? Explain.
7. What is the structure of Romans and the Heidelberg Catechism? Write it out in sentences.
8. What would you say to people who say they believe in TULIP but are cocky and ungodly?
9. What words would you pray to God in asking him to keep you humble?
10. Are these doctrines unimportant, sort of important, or very important? Explain.
11. In these lessons, what is one of the most amazing things you've learned?

MEMORY WORK

It is the LORD who goes before you. He will be with you; he will not leave you or forsake you. Do not fear or be dismayed. (Deut. 31:8)

Fear not, for I am with you; be not dismayed, for I am your God; I will strengthen you, I will help you, I will uphold you with my righteous right hand. (Isa. 41:10)

Appendix A

RECOMMENDED READING

The following books are those I've used to write the book you're holding or that I recommend. Most of these books are not overly difficult to read and study. If you are a teacher or leader of a group who is studying this book, I've put an asterisk (*) by the books below that would be most helpful for class preparation.

*Boice, James Montgomery, and Phillip Graham Ryken. *The Doctrines of Grace*. Wheaton: Crossway, 2009.

Brown, Craig. *The Five Dilemmas of Calvinism*. Orlando: Ligonier Ministries, 2007.

Calvin, John. *Institutes of the Christian Religion*. Louisville: Westminster John Knox, 1960.

De Jong, Peter Y., ed. *Crisis in the Reformed Churches: Essays in Commemoration of the Great Synod of Dort*. Grandville, MI: Reformed Fellowship, 2008.

Ferguson, Sinclair B. *The Christian Life: A Doctrinal Introduction*. Carlisle, PA: Banner of Truth, 1981.

Holstrom, Bryan. *The Gift of Faith*. Greenville, SC: Ambassador International, 2012.

Horton, Michael. *For Calvinism*. Grand Rapids: Zondervan, 2011.

Murray, John. *Redemption Accomplished and Applied*. Grand Rapids: Eerdmans, 1955.

*Palmer, Edwin. *The Five Points of Calvinism*. Grand Rapids: Baker, 1972.

*Phillips, Richard D. *What's So Great about the Doctrines of Grace?* Orlando: Reformation Trust, 2008.

Sproul, R. C. *Grace Unknown*. Grand Rapids: Baker, 1997.

*Steele, David N., Curtis C. Thomas, and Lance S. Quinn. *The Five Points of Calvinism*, 2nd ed. Phillipsburg, NJ: P&R Publishing, 2004.

*Venema, Cornelis. *But for the Grace of God: An Exposition of the Canons of Dort*. Grand Rapids: Reformed Fellowship, 1994.

Appendix B

TULIP IN THE CONFESSIONS

As we learned in the lessons, the doctrines of grace are found in the Reformed and Presbyterian confessions. Here is a basic list where these doctrines are clearly found in these confessions. *BCF* is the Belgic Confession of Faith, *COD* is the Canons of Dort, *HC* is the Heidelberg Catechism, *WCF* is the Westminster Confession of Faith, *WLC* is the Westminster Larger Catechism, and *WSC* is the Westminster Shorter Catechism.

TOTAL DEPRAVITY
COD III/IV
HC Q/A 5–14
BCF 14–15
WCF 6.1–6; 9.1–5; 16.7
WLC Q/A 21–29, 149
WSC Q/A 13–19, 82

UNCONDITIONAL ELECTION
COD I
BCF 16

HC Q/A 54
WCF 3.1–8; 7.3; 8.1; 10.1–3
WLC Q/A 12–14, 30–32
WSC Q/A 20

LIMITED (DEFINITE) ATONEMENT

BCF 16
COD II
HC Q/A 21, 54, 55
WCF 8.1, 5–6, 8; 11.4
WLC Q/A 44, 52, 59, 64
WSC Q/A 21

IRRESISTIBLE GRACE

COD III/IV
HC Q/A 65
BCF 22, 24
WCF 7.2; 8.8; 10.1–4; 13.1; 14.1
WLC Q/A 32, 59, 66–68, 154
WSC Q/A 30–31, 88–89

PERSEVERANCE (PRESERVATION) OF THE SAINTS

COD V
HC Q/A 1, 28, 31–32, 52–58
BCF 27, 37
WCF 11.5; 17.1–3; 33.2
WLC Q/A 45, 74, 79, 86, 90
WSC Q/A 36

Appendix C

SCRIPTURE INDEX

There are many stories and verses in the Old and New Testaments that teach the doctrines of grace. We haven't studied every verse in the Bible that talks about TULIP, but here is a list of the ones we did look at. For more Scripture references, refer to the books in the recommended reading list in appendix A and the proof texts found in the confessions listed in appendix B.

TOTAL DEPRAVITY
Genesis 6:5
Psalm 51:5
Psalm 143:2
Ecclesiastes 7:20
Ecclesiastes 9:3
Jeremiah 13:23
Jeremiah 17:9
Matthew 7:16–18
Mark 7:21–23
John 8:34, 44

Acts 8:23

Romans 3:10–12, 23

Romans 5:12, 18–19

Romans 6:20

Romans 8:8

Ephesians 2:1, 3

Ephesians 4:18

Titus 3:3

1 John 3:10, 12

UNCONDITIONAL ELECTION

Exodus 33:19

Deuteronomy 7:6

Psalm 33:12

Psalm 65:4

Psalm 106:5

Isaiah 44:1

Matthew 22:14

Matthew 24:22–24, 31

Mark 13:20–22, 27

John 13:18

John 15:16

John 17:12

Acts 9:15

Acts 13:48

Romans 9:10–13, 15–16, 18, 21

Romans 11:5–6

Ephesians 1:4–5, 11

Revelation 20:15

Revelation 21:27

LIMITED (DEFINITE) ATONEMENT

Isaiah 53:5–6

Ezekiel 34:11–12

Matthew 1:21

John 6:39

John 10:14–15, 28–29

John 17:2, 6–9

John 19:28, 30

Romans 5:8

Galatians 3:13

Ephesians 5:2, 25

Titus 2:14

1 Peter 3:18

1 John 3:16

IRRESISTIBLE GRACE

Isaiah 50:5

Isaiah 55:11

Ezekiel 36:26

Ezekiel 37:1–10

Luke 24:32

John 3:3

John 6:44, 63

John 10:14–16, 27

Acts 11:18

Acts 16:14

Romans 7:6

Romans 8:30

Romans 10:17

2 Corinthians 3:6

2 Corinthians 5:17–18

Ephesians 2:4–5

Titus 3:5

1 Peter 1:3

1 John 4:19

1 John 5:20

PERSEVERANCE (PRESERVATION) OF THE SAINTS

Deuteronomy 31:8

Psalm 23:6

Psalm 37:28

Psalm 40:11

Psalm 97:10

Psalm 138:8

Isaiah 41:10

Isaiah 43:25

Isaiah 54:10

Jeremiah 32:40

Luke 22:32

John 6:40

John 10:28–29

Romans 8:35–39

1 Corinthians 1:7–8

1 Corinthians 6:14

1 Corinthians 9:24–27

1 Corinthians 10:13

1 Corinthians 15:58

Galatians 6:9

Philippians 1:6

1 Thessalonians 2:12

2 Timothy 4:18
Hebrews 12:1
James 1:12
2 Peter 1:10
1 John 2:19

Appendix D

THE CANONS OF DORT

The Canons of Dort are a set of statements (canons) that were written as a response to unbiblical teaching within the Reformed church of Holland in the early seventeenth century. Some preachers and teachers taught these five points: (1) conditional election, (2) unlimited atonement, (3) partial depravity, (4) resistible grace, and (5) apostasy of true Christians.[1] The Synod of Dort in 1618–19 was called to deal with these errors. The result was a statement of five points that upheld the truths of Reformed doctrine and refuted the errors of the unbiblical teaching.[2] These points are explained in this order in the Canons of Dort: (1) unconditional election, (2) limited/definite atonement, (3) total depravity, (4) irresistible grace, and (5) perseverance/preservation of the saints.

Some people say it is theological nitpicking to discuss doctrine so meticulously. However, as becomes evident when reading the document, these are significant parts of the Christian faith that need to be discussed in detail. Historic Reformed

1. These teachers were called the Remonstrants. Today this teaching is best known as Arminian doctrine because one teacher of these points was Jacob Arminius.
2. These five points are called "points of doctrine" in the Canons of Dort and are divided into smaller articles.

churches believe that these truths in the Canons of Dort clearly showcase our triune God's sovereignty in salvation. These truths help Christians believe with more depth and conviction what Psalm 3:8 says: "Salvation belongs to the LORD."

The Canons of Dort can be summarized as a statement of faith in this way: (1) We believe that before the foundation of the world God chose to save sinners based on his good pleasure alone and not because of anything in them or done by them. (2) We believe that Christ died for his sheep, only those whom the Father chose before the foundation of the world. (3) We believe that by nature humans are born in sin and in bondage to sin; they do not have free will. (4) We believe that God's saving grace is irresistible. (5) We believe that those whom God has chosen, for whom Christ has died, who have been irresistibly changed by grace, will certainly be preserved by God to the end and will never fall away. These points have been called the "Five Points of Calvinism" or "TULIP," but a careful study will show that neither the Synod of Dort nor any teacher in the Protestant Reformation made up these truths—they are found in the Bible. Because these are important truths, historic Reformed churches hold tightly to these teachings as they seek to glorify God alone for his gracious work of saving sinners from the flames of hell.

THE CANONS OF DORT

I. Divine Election and Reprobation

1. As all men have sinned in Adam, lie under the curse, and are deserving of eternal death, God would have done no injustice by leaving them all to perish and delivering them over to condemnation on account of sin, according to the words of the

apostle, "that every mouth may be stopped, and all the world may become guilty before God" (Rom. 3:19); and "for all have sinned, and come short of the glory of God" (Rom. 3:23); and "for the wages of sin is death" (Rom. 6:23).

2. But in this the love of God was manifested, that he sent his only begotten Son into the world, that whosoever believeth on him should not perish, but have everlasting life (1 John 4:9; John 3:16).

3. And that men may be brought to believe, God mercifully sends the messengers of these most joyful tidings, to whom he will and at what time he pleaseth; by whose ministry men are called to repentance and faith in Christ crucified. "How then shall they call on him in whom they have not believed? and how shall they believe in him of whom they have not heard? and how shall they hear without a preacher? and how shall they preach, except they be sent?" (Rom. 10:14–15).

4. The wrath of God abideth on those who believe not this gospel. But such as receive it, and embrace Jesus the Savior by a true and living faith, are by him delivered from the wrath of God, and from destruction, and have the gift of eternal life conferred on them.

5. The cause or guilt of this unbelief as well as of all other sins, is no wise in God, but in man himself; whereas faith in Jesus Christ and salvation through him is the free gift of God, as it is written, "By grace ye are saved through faith; and that not of yourselves: it is the gift of God" (Eph. 2:8); and "for unto

you it is given in the behalf of Christ, not only to believe on him" (Phil. 1:29).

6. That some receive the gift of faith from God, and others do not receive it proceeds from God's eternal decree, "Known unto God are all his works from the beginning of the world" (Acts 15:18). "Who worketh all things after the counsel of his own will" (Eph. 1:11). According to which decree, he graciously softens the hearts of the elect, however obstinate, and inclines them to believe, while he leaves the nonelect in his just judgment to their own wickedness and obduracy. And herein is especially displayed the profound, and merciful, and at the same time the righteous discrimination between men, equally involved in ruin; or that decree of election and reprobation, revealed in the Word of God, which though men of perverse, impure, and unstable minds wrest to their own destruction, yet to holy and pious souls affords unspeakable consolation.

7. Election is the unchangeable purpose of God whereby, before the foundation of the world, he hath out of mere grace, according to the sovereign good pleasure of his own will, chosen, from the whole human race, which had fallen through their own fault from their primitive state of rectitude into sin and destruction, a certain number of persons to redemption in Christ, whom he from eternity appointed the mediator and head of the elect, and the foundation of salvation.

This elect number, though by nature neither better nor more deserving than the others, but with them involved in one common misery, God hath decreed to give to Christ, to be saved by him, and effectually to call and draw them to his communion by his Word and Spirit, to bestow on them true faith, justification, and sanctification; and having powerfully preserved them in the fellowship of his Son, finally, to glorify them for the demonstration of his mercy, and for the praise of his glorious grace; as it is written,

> According as he hath chosen us in him before the foundation of the world, that we should be holy and without blame before him in love: having predestinated us unto the adoption of children by Jesus Christ to himself, according to the good pleasure of his will, to the praise of the glory of his grace, wherein he hath made us accepted in the beloved. (Eph. 1:4–6)

And elsewhere, "Whom he did predestinate, them he also called: and whom he called, them he also justified: and whom he justified, them he also glorified" (Rom. 8:30).

8. There are not various decrees of election, but one and the same decree respecting all those who shall be saved, both under the Old and New Testament, since the Scripture declares the good pleasure, purpose, and counsel of the divine will to be one, according to which he hath chosen us from eternity, both to grace and glory, to salvation and the way of salvation, which he hath ordained that we should walk therein.

9. This election was not founded on foreseen faith, and the obedience of faith, holiness, or any other good quality of disposition in man, as the prerequisite, cause, or condition on which it depended; but men are chosen to faith and to the obedience of faith, holiness, etc., therefore election is

the fountain of every saving good, from which proceed faith, holiness, and the other gifts of salvation, and finally eternal life itself, as its fruits and effects, according to that of the apostle: "He hath chosen us . . . [not because we were, but] that we should be holy and without blame before him in love" (Eph. 1:4).

10. The good pleasure of God is the sole cause of this gracious election, which doth not consist herein, that out of all possible qualities and actions of men God has chosen some as a condition of salvation, but that he was pleased out of the common mass of sinners to adopt some certain persons as a peculiar people to himself, as it is written,

> (For the children being not yet born, neither having done any good or evil . . .) it was said unto her [namely to Rebekah], "The elder shall serve the younger." As it is written, "Jacob have I loved, but Esau have I hated." (Rom. 9:11–13)

"And as many as were ordained to eternal life believed" (Acts 13:48).

11. And as God himself is most wise, unchangeable, omniscient, and omnipotent, so the election made by him can neither be interrupted nor changed, recalled, or annulled; neither can the elect be cast away, nor their number diminished.

12. The elect in due time, though in various degrees and in different measures, attain the assurance of this their eternal and unchangeable election, not by inquisitively prying into the

secret and deep things of God, but by observing in themselves with a spiritual joy and holy pleasure the infallible fruits of election pointed out in the Word of God—such as a true faith in Christ, filial fear, a godly sorrow for sin, a hungering and thirsting after righteousness, etc.

13. The sense and certainty of this election afford to the children of God additional matter for daily humiliation before him, for adoring the depth of his mercies, for cleansing themselves, and rendering grateful returns of ardent love to him, who first manifested so great love towards them. The consideration of this doctrine of election is so far from encouraging remissness in the observance of the divine commands, or from sinking men in carnal security, that these, in the just judgment of God, are the usual effects of rash presumption, or of idle and wanton trifling with the grace of election, in those who refuse to walk in the ways of the elect.

14. As the doctrine of divine election by the most wise counsel of God, was declared by the prophets, by Christ himself, and by the apostles, and is clearly revealed in the Scriptures, both of the Old and New Testament, so it is still to be published in due time and place in the church of God, for which it was peculiarly designed, provided it be done with reverence, in the spirit of discretion and piety, for the glory of God's most holy name, and for enlivening and comforting his people, without vainly attempting to investigate the secret ways of the Most High (Acts 20:27; Rom. 11:33–34; 12:3; Heb. 6:17–18).

15. What peculiarly tends to illustrate and recommend to us the eternal and unmerited grace of election is the express testimony of sacred Scripture, that not all, but some only are elected, while others are passed by in the eternal election of God; whom God, out of his sovereign, most just, irreprehensible, and unchangeable good pleasure, hath decreed to leave in the common misery into which they have willfully plunged themselves, and not to bestow on them saving faith and the grace of conversion, but leaving them in his just judgment to follow their own ways, at last for the declaration of his justice, to condemn and punish them forever, not only on account of their unbelief, but also for all their other sins. And this is the decree of reprobation which by no means makes God the author of sin (the very thought of which is blasphemy), but declares him to be an awful, irreprehensible, and righteous judge and avenger thereof.

16. Those who do not yet experience a lively faith in Christ, an assured confidence of soul, peace of conscience, an earnest endeavor after filial obedience, and glorying in God through Christ, efficaciously wrought in them, and do nevertheless persist in the use of the means which God hath appointed for working these graces in us, ought not to be alarmed at the mention of reprobation, nor to rank themselves among the reprobate, but diligently to persevere in the use of means, and with ardent desires, devoutly and humbly to wait for a season of richer grace. Much less cause have they to be terrified by the doctrine of reprobation, who, though they seriously desire to be turned to God, to please him only, and to be delivered from the body of death, cannot yet reach that measure of

holiness and faith to which they aspire; since a merciful God has promised that he will not quench the smoking flax, nor break the bruised reed. But this doctrine is justly terrible to those, who, regardless of God and of the Savior Jesus Christ, have wholly given themselves up to the cares of the world and the pleasures of the flesh, so long as they are not seriously converted to God.

17. Since we are to judge of the will of God from his Word, which testifies that the children of believers are holy, not by nature, but in virtue of the covenant of grace in which they, together with the parents, are comprehended, godly parents have no reason to doubt of the election and salvation of their children, whom it pleaseth God to call out of this life in their infancy.

18. To those who murmur at the free grace of election and just severity of reprobation, we answer with the apostle, "Nay but, O man, who art thou that repliest against God?" (Rom. 9:20), and quote the language of our Savior: "Is it not lawful for me to do what I will with mine own?" (Matt. 20:15). And therefore with holy adoration of these mysteries, we exclaim in the words of the apostle:

> O the depth of the riches both of the wisdom and knowledge of God! how unsearchable are his judgments, and his ways past finding out! For who hath known the mind of the Lord? or who hath been his counsellor? or who hath first given to him, and it shall be recompensed unto him again? For of him, and through him, and to him, are all things: to whom be glory for ever. Amen. (Rom. 11:33–36)

The true doctrine concerning election and reprobation having been explained, the Synod rejects the errors of those:

1. who teach that the will of God to save those who would believe and would persevere in faith and in the obedience of faith, is the whole and entire decree of election unto salvation, and that nothing else concerning this decree has been revealed in God's Word.

For these deceive the simple and plainly contradict the Scriptures, which declare that God will not only save those who will believe, but that he has also from eternity chosen certain particular persons to whom above others he in time will grant both faith in Christ and perseverance; as it written: "I have manifested thy name unto the men which thou gavest me out of the world" (John 17:6); "And as many as were ordained to eternal life believed" (Acts 13:48); and "according as he chose us in him before the foundation of the world, that we should be holy and without blame before him in love" (Eph. 1:4).

2. who teach that there are various kinds of election of God unto eternal life—the one general and indefinite, the other particular and definite—and that the latter in turn is either incomplete, revocable, nondecisive, and conditional, or complete, irrevocable, decisive, and absolute. Likewise, that there is one election unto faith, and another unto salvation, so that election can be unto justifying faith, without being a decisive election unto salvation. For this is a fancy of men's minds, invented regardless of the Scriptures, whereby the doctrine of election is corrupted, and this golden chain of our salvation is

broken. "Whom he did predestinate, them he also called: and whom he called, them he also justified: and whom he justified, them he also glorified" (Rom. 8:30).

3. who teach that the good pleasure and purpose of God, of which Scripture makes mention in the doctrine of election, does not consist in this, that God chose certain persons rather than others, but in this that he chose out of all possible conditions (among which are also the works of the law), or out of the whole order of things, the act of faith which from its very nature is undeserving, as well as its incomplete obedience, as a condition of salvation, and that he would graciously consider this in itself as a complete obedience and count it worthy of the reward of eternal life. For by this injurious error the pleasure of God and the merits of Christ are made of none effect, and men are drawn away by useless questions from the truth of gracious justification and from the simplicity of Scripture, and this declaration of the apostle is charged as untrue: "Who hath saved us, and called us with an holy calling, not according to our works, but according to his own purpose and grace, which was given us in Christ Jesus before the world began" (2 Tim. 1:9).

4. who teach that in the election unto faith this condition is beforehand demanded; namely, that man should use the light of nature aright, be pious, humble, meek, and fit for eternal life, as if on these things election were in any way dependent. For this savors of the teaching of Pelagius, and is opposed to the doctrine of the apostle when he writes,

Among whom also we all had our conversation in times past in the lusts of our flesh, fulfilling the desires of the flesh and of the mind; and were by nature the children of wrath, even as others. But God, who is rich in mercy, for his great love wherewith he loved us, even when we were dead in sins, hath quickened us together with Christ, (by grace ye are saved;) and hath raised us up together, and made us sit together in heavenly places in Christ Jesus: that in the ages to come he might shew the exceeding riches of his grace in his kindness toward us through Christ Jesus. For by grace are ye saved through faith; and that not of yourselves: it is the gift of God: not of works, lest any man should boast. (Eph. 2:3–9)

5. who teach that the incomplete and nondecisive election of particular persons to salvation occurred because of a foreseen faith, conversion, holiness, godliness, which either began or continued for some time; but that the complete and decisive election occurred because of foreseen perseverance unto the end in faith, conversion, holiness, and godliness; and that this is the gracious and evangelical worthiness, for the sake of which he who is chosen is more worthy than he who is not chosen; and that therefore faith, the obedience of faith, holiness, godliness, and perseverance are not fruits of the unchangeable election unto glory, but are conditions which, being required beforehand, were foreseen as being met by those who will be fully elected, and are causes without which the unchangeable election to glory does not occur.

This is repugnant to the entire Scripture, which constantly inculcates this and similar declarations: election is "not of works, but of him that calleth" (Rom. 9:11). "As many as were ordained to eternal life believed" (Acts 13:48). "He hath chosen us in him before the foundation of the world, that we should be holy" (Eph. 1:4). "Ye have not chosen me, but I have chosen you" (John 15:16). "And if by grace, then is it no more of works" (Rom. 11:6). "Herein is love, not that we loved God, but that he loved us, and sent his Son" (1 John 4:10).

6. who teach that not every election unto salvation is unchangeable, but that some of the elect, any decree of God notwithstanding, can yet perish and do indeed perish. By which gross error they make God to be changeable, and destroy the comfort which the godly obtain out of the firmness of their election, and contradict the Holy Scripture, which teaches that the elect cannot be lead astray (Matt. 24:24); that Christ does not lose those whom the Father gave him (John 6:39); and that God hath also glorified those whom he foreordained, called, and justified (Rom. 8:30).

7. who teach that there is in this life no fruit and no consciousness of the unchangeable election to glory, nor any certainty, except that which depends on a changeable and uncertain condition. For not only is it absurd to speak of an uncertain certainty, but also contrary to the experience of the saints, who by virtue of the consciousness of their election rejoice with the apostle and praise this favor of God (Eph. 1); who according to Christ's admonition rejoice with his disciples that their names are written in heaven (Luke 10:20); who also place the consciousness of their election over against the fiery darts of the Devil, asking,

"Who shall lay any thing to the charge of God's elect?" (Rom. 8:33).

8. who teach that God, simply by virtue of his righteous will, did not decide either to leave anyone in the fall of Adam and in the common state of sin and condemnation, or to pass anyone by in the communication of grace which is necessary for faith and conversion. For this is firmly decreed: "Therefore hath he mercy on whom he will have mercy, and whom he will he hardeneth" (Rom. 9:18). And also this: "It is given unto you to know the mysteries of the kingdom of heaven, but to them it is not given" (Matt. 13:11). Likewise, "I thank thee, O Father, Lord of heaven and earth, because thou hast hid these things from the wise and prudent, and hast revealed them unto babes. Even so, Father: for so it seemed good in thy sight" (Matt. 11:25–26).

9. who teach that the reason why God sends the gospel to one people rather than to another is not merely and solely the good pleasure of God, but rather the fact that one people is better and worthier than another to whom the gospel is not communicated. For this Moses denies, addressing the people of Israel as follows:

> Behold, the heaven and the heaven of heavens is the Lord's thy God, the earth also, with all that therein is. Only the Lord had a delight in thy fathers to love them, and he chose their seed after them, even you above all people, as it is this day. (Deut. 10:14–15)

And Christ said, "Woe unto thee, Chorazin! woe unto thee, Bethsaida! for if the mighty works, which were done in you, had been done in Tyre and Sidon, they would have repented long ago in sackcloth and ashes" (Matt. 11:21).

II. Of the Death of Christ, and the Redemption of Men Thereby

1. God is not only supremely merciful, but also supremely just. And his justice requires (as he hath revealed himself in his Word) that our sins committed against his infinite majesty should be punished, not only with temporal but with eternal punishment, both in body and soul; which we cannot escape, unless satisfaction be made to the justice of God.

2. Since therefore we are unable to make that satisfaction in our own persons, or to deliver ourselves from the wrath of God, he hath been pleased in his infinite mercy to give his only begotten Son, for our surety, who was made sin and became a curse for us and in our stead, that he might make satisfaction to divine justice on our behalf.

3. The death of the Son of God is the only and most perfect sacrifice and satisfaction for sin, and is of infinite worth and value, abundantly sufficient to expiate the sins of the whole world.

4. This death derives its infinite value and dignity from these considerations, because the person who submitted to it was not only really man and perfectly holy, but also the only begotten Son of God, of the same eternal and infinite essence with the

Father and the Holy Spirit, which qualifications were necessary to constitute him a Savior for us, and because it was attended with a sense of the wrath and curse of God due to us for sin.

5. Moreover, the promise of the gospel is that whosoever believeth in Christ crucified shall not perish but have everlasting life. This promise, together with the command to repent and believe, ought to be declared and published to all nations, and to all persons promiscuously and without distinction, to whom God out of his good pleasure sends the gospel.

6. And whereas many who are called by the gospel do not repent nor believe in Christ, but perish in unbelief, this is not owing to any defect or insufficiency in the sacrifice offered by Christ on the cross, but is wholly to be imputed to themselves.

7. But as many as truly believe, and are delivered and saved from sin and destruction through the death of Christ, are indebted for this benefit solely to the grace of God, given them in Christ from everlasting, and not to any merit of their own.

8. For this was the sovereign counsel and most gracious will and purpose of God the Father, that the quickening and saving efficacy of the most precious death of his Son should extend to all the elect, for bestowing on them alone the gift of justifying faith, thereby to bring them infallibly to salvation: that is, it was the will of God that Christ by the blood of the cross, whereby he confirmed the new covenant, should effectually redeem out of every people, tribe, nation, and language all those, and those only, who were from eternity chosen to sal-

vation and given to him by the Father; that he should confer on them faith, which together with all the other saving gifts of the Holy Spirit, he purchased for them by his death; should purge them from all sin, both original and actual, whether committed before or after believing; and having faithfully preserved them even to the end, should at last bring them free from every spot and blemish to the enjoyment of glory in his own presence forever.

9. This purpose proceeding from everlasting love towards the elect has from the beginning of the world to this day been powerfully accomplished, and will henceforward still continue to be accomplished, notwithstanding all the ineffectual opposition of the gates of hell, so that the elect in due time may be gathered together into one, and that there never may be wanting a church composed of believers, the foundation of which is laid in the blood of Christ, which may steadfastly love and faithfully serve him as their Savior who, as a bridegroom for his bride, laid down his life for them on the cross, and which may celebrate his praises here and through all eternity.

The true doctrine having been explained, the Synod rejects the errors of those:

1. who teach that God the Father has ordained his Son to the death of the cross without a certain and definite decree to save any, so that the necessity, profitableness, and worth of what Christ merited by his death might have existed, and might remain in all its parts complete, perfect, and intact, even if the merited redemption had never in fact been applied to any

person. For this doctrine tends to the despising of the wisdom of the Father and of the merits of Jesus Christ, and is contrary to Scripture. For thus saith our Savior: "I lay down my life for the sheep," and "I know them" (John 10:15, 27). And the prophet Isaiah saith concerning the Savior, "When thou shalt make his soul an offering for sin, he shall see his seed, he shall prolong his days, and the pleasure of the LORD shall prosper in his hand" (Isa. 53:10). Finally, this contradicts the article of faith according to which we believe the catholic Christian church.

2. who teach that it was not the purpose of the death of Christ that he should confirm the new covenant of grace through his blood, but only that he should acquire for the Father the mere right to establish with man such a covenant as he might please, whether of grace or of works. For this is repugnant to Scripture, which teaches that Christ has become the surety and mediator of a better, that is, the new covenant, and that a testament is of force where death has occurred (Heb. 7:22; 9:15, 17).

3. who teach that Christ by his satisfaction merited neither salvation itself for anyone, nor faith, whereby this satisfaction of Christ unto salvation is effectually appropriated; but that he merited for the Father only the authority or the perfect will to deal again with man, and to prescribe new conditions as he might desire, obedience to which, however, depended on the free will of man, so that it therefore might have come to pass that either none or all should fulfill these conditions. For these adjudge too contemptuously of the death of Christ, do

in no wise acknowledge the most important fruit or benefit thereby gained, and bring again out of hell the Pelagian error.

4. who teach that the new covenant of grace, which God the Father through the mediation of the death of Christ made with man, does not herein consist that we by faith, inasmuch as it accepts the merits of Christ, are justified before God and saved, but in the fact that God, having revoked the demand of perfect obedience of the law, regards faith itself and the obedience of faith, although imperfect, as the perfect obedience of the law, and does esteem it worthy of the reward of eternal life through grace. For these contradict the Scriptures: "Being justified freely by his grace through the redemption that is in Christ Jesus: whom God hath set forth to be a propitiation through faith in his blood" (Rom. 3:24–25). And these proclaim, as did the wicked Socinus, a new and strange justification of man before God, against the consensus of the whole church.

5. who teach that all men have been accepted unto the state of reconciliation and unto the grace of the covenant, so that no one is worthy of condemnation on account of original sin, and that no one shall be condemned because of it, but that all are free from the guilt of original sin. For this opinion is repugnant to Scripture, which teaches that we are by nature children of wrath (Eph. 2:3).

6. who use the difference between meriting and appropriating, to the end that they may instill into the minds of the imprudent and inexperienced this teaching that God, as far as he is concerned, has been minded of applying to all equally the

benefits gained by the death of Christ; but that, while some obtain the pardon of sin and eternal life, and others do not, this difference depends on their own free will, which joins itself to the grace that is offered without exception, and that it is not dependent on the special gift of mercy, which powerfully works in them, that they rather than others should appropriate unto themselves this grace. For these, while they feign that they present this distinction, in a sound sense, seek to instill into the people the destructive poison of the Pelagian errors.

7. who teach that Christ neither could die, needed to die, nor did die for those whom God loved in the highest degree and elected to eternal life, and did not die for these, since these do not need the death of Christ. For they contradict the apostle, who declares, "[Christ] loved me, and gave himself for me" (Gal. 2:20). Likewise, "Who shall lay any thing to the charge of God's elect? It is God that justifieth. Who is he that condemneth? It is Christ Jesus that died" (Rom. 8:33–34), namely, for them; and the Savior who says, "I lay down my life for the sheep" (John 10:15); and

> This is my commandment, that ye love one another, as I have loved you. Greater love hath no man than this, that a man lay down his life for his friends. (John 15:12–13)

III/IV. Of the Corruption of Man, His Conversion to God, and the Manner Thereof

1. Man was originally formed after the image of God. His understanding was adorned with a true and saving knowledge of his Creator, and of spiritual things; his heart and will were

upright; all his affections pure; and the whole man was holy; but revolting from God by the instigation of the Devil, and abusing the freedom of his own will, he forfeited these excellent gifts; and on the contrary entailed on himself blindness of mind, horrible darkness, vanity, and perverseness of judgment, became wicked, rebellious, and obdurate in heart and will, and impure in his affections.

2. Man after the fall begat children in his own likeness. A corrupt stock produced a corrupt offspring. Hence all the posterity of Adam, Christ only excepted, have derived corruption from their original parent, not by imitation, as the Pelagians of old asserted, but by the propagation of a vicious nature.

3. Therefore all men are conceived in sin and by nature children of wrath, incapable of saving good, prone to evil, dead in sin, and in bondage thereto, and without the regenerating grace of the Holy Spirit they are neither able nor willing to return to God, to reform the depravity of their nature, nor to dispose themselves to reformation.

4. There remain, however, in man since the fall, the glimmerings of natural light, whereby he retains some knowledge of God, of natural things, and of the differences between good and evil, and discovers some regard for virtue, good order in society, and for maintaining an orderly external deportment. But so far is this light of nature from being sufficient to bring him to a saving knowledge of God, and to true conversion, that he is incapable of using it aright even in things natural and civil. Nay further, this light, such as it is, man in various

ways renders wholly polluted and holds it in unrighteousness, by doing which he becomes inexcusable before God.

5. In the same light are we to consider the law of the decalogue, delivered by God to his peculiar people the Jews by the hands of Moses. For though it discovers the greatness of sin, and more and more convinces man thereof, yet as it neither points out a remedy, nor imparts strength to extricate him from misery, and thus being weak through the flesh, leaves the transgressor under the curse, man cannot by this law obtain saving grace.

6. What therefore neither the light of nature nor the law could do, that God performs by the operation of the Holy Spirit through the word or ministry of reconciliation, which is the glad tidings concerning the Messiah, by means whereof it hath pleased God to save such as believe, as well under the Old as under the New Testament.

7. This mystery of his will God discovered to but a small number under the Old Testament; under the New (the distinction between various peoples having been removed) he reveals himself to many, without any distinction of people. The cause of this dispensation is not to be ascribed to the superior worth of one nation above another, nor to their making a better use of the light of nature, but results wholly from the sovereign good pleasure and unmerited love of God. Hence they, to whom so great and so gracious a blessing is communicated, above their desert, or rather notwithstanding their demerits, are bound to acknowledge it with humble and grateful hearts, and with

the apostle to adore, not curiously to pry into the severity and justice of God's judgments displayed to others, to whom this grace is not given.

8. As many as are called by the gospel are unfeignedly called. For God hath most earnestly and truly shown in his Word what is pleasing to him; namely, that those who are called should come to him. He, moreover, seriously promises eternal life and rest to as many as shall come to him and believe on him.

9. It is not the fault of the gospel, nor of Christ, offered therein, nor of God, who calls men by the gospel and confers on them various gifts, that those who are called by the ministry of the Word, refuse to come and be converted; the fault lies in themselves, some of whom when called, regardless of their danger, reject the word of life; others, though they receive it, suffer it not to make a lasting impression on their heart; therefore their joy, arising only from a temporary faith, soon vanishes and they fall away; while others choke the seed of the word by perplexing cares and the pleasures of this world and produce no fruit. This our Savior teaches in the parable of the sower (Matt. 13).

10. But that others who are called by the gospel obey the call and are converted is not to be ascribed to the proper exercise of free will, whereby one distinguishes himself above others, equally furnished with grace sufficient for faith and conversions, as the proud heresy of Pelagius maintains; but it must be wholly ascribed to God, who as he has chosen his own from eternity in Christ, so he confers on them faith and repentance,

rescues them from the power of darkness, and translates them into the kingdom of his own Son, that they may show forth the praises of him who hath called them out of darkness into his marvelous light, and may glory not in themselves but in the Lord, according to the testimony of the apostles in various places.

11. But when God accomplishes his good pleasure in the elect or works in them true conversion, he not only causes the gospel to be externally preached to them, and powerfully illumines their minds by his Holy Spirit, that they may rightly understand and discern the things of the Spirit of God; but by the efficacy of the same regenerating Spirit pervades the inmost recesses of the man, he opens the closed, and softens the hardened heart, and circumcises that which was uncircumcised, infuses new qualities into the will, which though heretofore dead he quickens; from being evil, disobedient, and refractory, he renders it good, obedient, and pliable; actuates and strengthens it, that like a good tree it may bring forth the fruits of good actions.

12. And this is the regeneration so highly celebrated in Scripture and denominated a new creation: a resurrection from the dead, a making alive, which God works in us without our aid. But this is in no wise effected merely by the external preaching of the gospel, by moral suasion, or such a mode of operation, that after God has performed his part, it still remains in the power of man to be regenerated or not, to be converted or to continue unconverted; but it is evidently a supernatural work, most powerful, and at the same time most delightful, astonishing, mysterious, and ineffable; not inferior in efficacy

to creation or the resurrection from the dead, as the Scripture inspired by the author of this work declares; so that all in whose heart God works in this marvelous manner are certainly, infallibly, and effectually regenerated and do actually believe. Whereupon the will thus renewed is not only actuated and influenced by God, but in consequence of this influence becomes itself active. Wherefore also man is himself rightly said to believe and repent, by virtue of that grace received.

13. The manner of this operation cannot be fully comprehended by believers in this life. Notwithstanding which, they rest satisfied with knowing and experiencing that by this grace of God they are enabled to believe with the heart and love their Savior.

14. Faith is therefore to be considered as the gift of God, not on account of its being offered by God to man, to be accepted or rejected at his pleasure; but because it is in reality conferred, breathed, and infused into him; or even because God bestows the power or ability to believe, and then expects that man should by the exercise of his own free will consent to the terms of that salvation and actually believe in Christ; but because he who works in man both to will and to do, and indeed all things in all, produces both the will to believe and the act of believing also.

15. God is under no obligation to confer this grace on any; for how can he be indebted to man, who had no precious gifts to bestow, as a foundation for such recompense? Nay, who has nothing of his own but sin and falsehood? He therefore

who becomes the subject of this grace owes eternal gratitude to God and gives him thanks forever. Whoever is not made partaker thereof is either altogether regardless of these spiritual gifts and satisfied with his own condition or is in no apprehension of danger and vainly boasts the possession of that which he has not. With respect to those who make an external profession of faith and live regular lives, we are bound, after the example of the apostle, to judge and speak of them in the most favorable manner. For the secret recesses of the heart are unknown to us. And as to others who have not yet been called, it is our duty to pray for them to God, who calls the things that are not as if they were. But we are in no wise to conduct ourselves towards them with haughtiness, as if we had made ourselves to differ.

16. But as man by the fall did not cease to be a creature, endowed with understanding and will, nor did sin, which pervaded the whole race of mankind, deprive him of the human nature, but brought on him depravity and spiritual death; so also this grace of regeneration does not treat men as senseless stocks and blocks, nor take away their will and its properties, neither does violence thereto, but spiritually quickens, heals, corrects, and at the same time sweetly and powerfully bends it; that where carnal rebellion and resistance formerly prevailed, a ready and sincere spiritual obedience begins to reign, in which the true and spiritual restoration and freedom of our will consist. Wherefore unless the admirable author of every good work wrought in us, man could have no hope of recovering from his fall by his own free will, by the abuse of which, in a state of innocence, he plunged himself into ruin.

17. As the almighty operation of God, whereby he prolongs and supports this our natural life, does not exclude but requires the use of means, by which God of his infinite mercy and goodness hath chosen to exert his influence, so also the before-mentioned supernatural operation of God, by which we are regenerated, in no wise excludes or subverts the use of the gospel, which the most wise God has ordained to be the seed of regeneration and food of the soul. Wherefore, as the apostles, and teachers who succeeded them, piously instructed the people concerning this grace of God, to his glory, and the abasement of all pride, and in the meantime, however, neglected not to keep them by the sacred precepts of the gospel in the exercise of the Word, sacraments, and discipline; so even to this day, be it far from either instructors or instructed to presume to tempt God in the church by separating what he of his good pleasure hath most intimately joined together. For grace is conferred by means of admonitions, and the more readily we perform our duty, the more eminent usually is this blessing of God working in us, and the more directly is his work advanced; to whom alone all the glory both of means and of their saving fruit and efficacy is forever due. Amen.

The true doctrine having been explained, the Synod rejects the errors of those:

1. who teach that it cannot properly be said that original sin in itself suffices to condemn the whole human race or to deserve temporal and eternal punishment. For these contradict the apostle who declares, "Wherefore, as by one man sin entered into the world, and death by sin; and so death passed upon all men, for that all have sinned" (Rom. 5:12); and "the judgment

was by one to condemnation" (Rom. 5:16); and "the wages of sin is death" (Rom. 6:23).

2. who teach that the spiritual gifts or the good qualities and virtues, such as goodness, holiness, righteousness, could not belong to the will of man when he was first created, and that these, therefore, could not have been separated therefrom in the fall. For such is contrary to the description of the image of God, which the apostle gives in Ephesians 4:24, where he declares that it consists in righteousness and holiness, which undoubtedly belong to the will.

3. who teach that in spiritual death the spiritual gifts are not separate from the will of man, since the will in itself has never been corrupted, but only hindered through the darkness of the understanding and the irregularity of the affections; and that, these hindrances having been removed, the will can then bring into operation its native powers; that is, that the will of itself is able to will and to choose, or not to will and not to choose, all manner of good which may be presented to it. This is an innovation and an error and tends to elevate the powers of the free will, contrary to the declaration of the prophet: "The heart is deceitful above all things, and desperately wicked" (Jer. 17:9); and of the apostle: "Among whom [children of disobedience] also we all had our conversation in times past in the lusts of our flesh, fulfilling the desires of the flesh and of the mind" (Eph. 2:3).

4. who teach that the unregenerate man is not really nor utterly dead in sin, nor destitute of all powers unto spiritual good, but that he can yet hunger and thirst after righteousness and life,

and offer the sacrifice of a contrite and broken spirit, which is pleasing to God. For these are contrary to the express testimony of Scripture. "You . . . were dead in trespasses and sins" (Eph. 2:1); and "Every imagination of the thoughts of his heart was only evil continually" (Gen. 6:5).

Moreover, to hunger and thirst after deliverance from misery, and after life, and to offer unto God the sacrifice of a broken spirit, is peculiar to the regenerate and those that are called blessed (Ps. 51:10, 19; Matt. 5:6).

5. who teach that the corrupt and natural man can so well use the common grace (by which they understand the light of nature), or the gifts still left him after the fall, that he can gradually gain by their good use a greater, namely, the evangelical or saving grace and salvation itself; and that in this way God on his part shows himself ready to reveal Christ unto all men, since he applies to all sufficiently and efficiently the means necessary to conversion. For the experience of all ages and the Scriptures do both testify that this is untrue. "He showeth his word unto Jacob, his statues and his judgments unto Israel. He hath not dealt so with any nation: and as for his judgments, they have not known them" (Ps. 147:19–20); and "Who in times past suffered all nations to walk in their own ways" (Acts 14:16); and "[Paul and his companions] were forbidden of the Holy Ghost to preach the word in Asia, after they were come to Mysia, they assayed to go into Bithynia: but the Spirit suffered them not" (Acts 16:6–7).

6. who teach that in the true conversion of man no new qualities, powers, or gifts can be infused by God into the will, and

that therefore faith through which we are first converted, and because of which we are called believers, is not a quality or gift infused by God but only an act of man, and that it cannot be said to be a gift, except in respect of the power to attain to this faith. For thereby they contradict the Holy Scriptures, which declare that God infuses new qualities of faith, of obedience, and of the consciousness of his love into our hearts: "I will put my law in their inward parts, and write it in their hearts" (Jer. 31:33); and "I will pour water upon him that is thirsty, and floods upon the dry ground: I will pour my spirit upon thy seed" (Isa. 44:3); and "The love of God is shed abroad in our hearts by the Holy Spirit which is given unto us" (Rom. 5:5). This is also repugnant to the continuous practice of the church, which prays by the mouth of the prophet thus: "Turn thou me, and I shall be turned" (Jer. 31:18).

7. who teach that the grace whereby we are converted to God is only a gentle advising or (as others explain it) that this is the noblest manner of working in the conversion of man, and that this manner of working, which consists in advising, is most in harmony with man's nature; and that there is no reason why this advising grace alone should not be sufficient to make the natural man spiritual; indeed, that God does not produce the consent of the will except through this manner of advising; and that the power of the divine working, whereby it surpasses the working of Satan, consists in this, that God promises eternal while Satan promises only temporal goods. But this is altogether Pelagian and contrary to the whole Scripture which, besides this, teaches another and far more powerful and divine manner of the Holy Spirit's working in

the conversion of man, as in Ezekiel: "A new heart also will I give you, and a new spirit will I put within you: and I will take away the stony heart out of your flesh, and I will give you an heart of flesh" (Ezek. 36:26).

8. who teach that God in the regeneration of man does not use such powers of his omnipotence as potently and infallibly bend man's will to faith and conversion; but that all the works of grace having been accomplished, which God employs to convert man, man may yet so resist God and the Holy Spirit, when God intends man's regeneration and wills to regenerate him, and indeed that man often does so resist that he prevents entirely his regeneration, and that it therefore remains in man's power to be regenerated or not. For this is nothing less than the denial of all the efficiency of God's grace in our conversion, and the subjecting of the working of Almighty God to the will of man, which is contrary to the apostles, who teach that we "believe, according to the working of his mighty power" (Eph. 1:19); and that God fulfills "all the good pleasure of his goodness, and the work of faith with power" (2 Thess. 1:11); and that "his divine power hath given unto us all things that pertain unto life and godliness" (2 Peter 1:3).

9. who teach that grace and free will are partial causes, which together work the beginning of conversion, and that grace, in order of working, does not precede the working of the will; that is, that God does not efficiently help the will of man unto conversion until the will of man moves and determines to do this. For the ancient church has long ago condemned this doctrine of the Pelagians according to the words of the

apostle: "So then it is not of him that willeth, nor of him that runneth, but of God that sheweth mercy" (Rom. 9:16). Likewise, "For who maketh thee to differ from another? and what hast thou that thou didst not receive?" (1 Cor. 4:7); and "For it is God which worketh in you both to will and to do of his good pleasure" (Phil. 2:13).

V. Of the Perseverance of the Saints

1. Whom God calls, according to his purpose, to the communion of his Son, our Lord Jesus Christ, and regenerates by the Holy Spirit, he delivers also from the dominion and slavery of sin in this life, though not altogether from the body of sin and from the infirmities of the flesh, so long as they continue in this world.

2. Hence spring daily sins of infirmity, and hence spots adhere to the best works of the saints; which furnish them with constant matter for humiliation before God and flying for refuge to Christ crucified; for mortifying the flesh more and more by the spirit of prayer and by holy exercises of piety; and for pressing forward to the goal of perfection, till being at length delivered from this body of death they are brought to reign with the Lamb of God in heaven.

3. By reason of these remains of indwelling sin and the temptations of sin and of the world, those who are converted could not persevere in a state of grace if left to their own strength. But God is faithful, who having conferred grace, mercifully confirms and powerfully preserves them herein, even to the end.

4. Although the weakness of the flesh cannot prevail against the power of God, who confirms and preserves true believers in a state of grace, yet converts are not always so influenced and actuated by the Spirit of God, as not in some particular instances sinfully to deviate from the guidance of divine grace, so as to be seduced by and to comply with the lusts of the flesh; they must therefore be constant in watching and in prayer that they be not led into temptation. When these are neglected, they are not only liable to be drawn into great and heinous sins by Satan, the world, and the flesh, but sometimes by the righteous permission of God actually fall into these evils. This, the lamentable fall of David, Peter, and other saints described in Holy Scripture, demonstrates.

5. By such enormous sins, however, they very highly offend God, incur a deadly guilt, grieve the Holy Spirit, interrupt the exercise of faith, very grievously wound their consciences, and sometimes lose the sense of God's favor for a time until, on their returning into the right way of serious repentance, the light of God's fatherly countenance again shines on them.

6. But God, who is rich in mercy, according to his unchangeable purpose of election, does not wholly withdraw the Holy Spirit from his own people, even in their melancholy falls; nor suffers them to proceed so far as to lose the grace of adoption and forfeit the state of justification or to commit sins unto death; nor does he permit them to be totally deserted and to plunge themselves into everlasting destruction.

7. For in the first place, in these falls he preserves them in the incorruptible seed of regeneration from perishing or being

totally lost; and again, by his Word and Spirit, certainly and effectually renews them to repentance, to a sincere and godly sorrow for their sins, that they may seek and obtain remission in the blood of the mediator, may again experience the favor of a reconciled God, through faith adore his mercies, and henceforward more diligently work out their own salvation with fear and trembling.

8. Thus it is not in consequence of their own merits or strength, but of God's free mercy, that they do not totally fall from faith and grace, nor continue and perish finally in their backslidings; which, with respect to themselves, is not only possible, but would undoubtedly happen; but with respect to God, it is utterly impossible, since his counsel cannot be changed, nor his promise fail, neither can the call according to his purpose be revoked, nor the merit, intercession, and preservation of Christ be rendered ineffectual, nor the sealing of the Holy Spirit be frustrated or obliterated.

9. Of this preservation of the elect to salvation, and of their perseverance in the faith, true believers for themselves may and ought to obtain assurance according to the measure of their faith, whereby they arrive at the certain persuasion that they ever will continue true and living members of the church, and that they experience forgiveness of sins, and will at last inherit eternal life.

10. This assurance, however, is not produced by any peculiar revelation contrary to or independent of the Word of God, but springs from faith in God's promises, which he has most

abundantly revealed in his Word for our comfort; from the testimony of the Holy Spirit, witnessing with our spirit that we are children and heirs of God (Rom. 8:16); and lastly, from a serious and holy desire to preserve a good conscience and to perform good works. And if the elect of God were deprived of this solid comfort, that they shall finally obtain the victory, and of this infallible pledge or earnest of eternal glory, they would be of all men the most miserable.

11. The Scripture moreover testifies that believers in this life have to struggle with various carnal doubts, and that under grievous temptations they are not always sensible of this full assurance of faith and certainty of persevering. But God, who is the Father of all consolation, does not suffer them to be tempted above that they are able, but will with the temptation also make a way to escape, that they may be able to bear it (1 Cor. 10:13), and by the Holy Spirit again inspires them with the comfortable assurance of persevering.

12. This certainty of perseverance, however, is so far from exciting in believers a spirit of pride, or of rendering them carnally secure, that on the contrary, it is the real source of humility, filial reverence, true piety, patience in every tribulation, fervent prayers, constancy in suffering, and in confessing the truth, and of solid rejoicing in God, so that the consideration of this benefit should serve as an incentive to the serious and constant practice of gratitude and good works, as appears from the testimonies of Scripture and the examples of the saints.

13. Neither does renewed confidence or persevering produce licentiousness, or a disregard to piety in those who are recovering from backsliding, but it renders them much more careful and solicitous to continue in the ways of the Lord, which he hath ordained, that they who walk therein may maintain an assurance of persevering, lest by abusing his fatherly kindness God should turn away his gracious countenance from them, to behold which is to the godly dearer than life; the withdrawing thereof is more bitter than death, and they in consequence hereof should fall into more grievous torments of conscience.

14. And as it hath pleased God, by the preaching of the gospel, to begin this work of grace in us, so he preserves, continues, and perfects it by the hearing and reading of his Word, by meditation thereon, and by the exhortations, threatenings, and promises thereof, as well as by the use of the sacraments.

15. The carnal mind is unable to comprehend this doctrine of the perseverance of the saints and the certainty thereof, which God hath most abundantly revealed in his Word for the glory of his name and the consolation of pious souls, and which he impresses on the hearts of the faithful. Satan abhors it, the world ridicules it, the ignorant and hypocrite abuse it, and heretics oppose it, but the spouse of Christ hath always most tenderly loved and constantly defended it as an inestimable treasure; and God, against whom neither counsel nor strength can prevail, will dispose her to continue this conduct to the end. Now to this one God, Father, Son, and Holy Spirit, be honor and glory forever. Amen.

The true doctrine having been explained, the Synod rejects the errors of those:

1. who teach that the perseverance of the true believers is not a fruit of election or a gift of God, gained by the death of Christ, but a condition of the new covenant, which (as they declare) man before his decisive election and justification must fulfill through his free will. For the Holy Scripture testifies that this follows out of election and is given the elect in virtue of the death, resurrection, and intercession of Christ: "But the election hath obtained it, and the rest were blinded" (Rom. 11:7). Likewise,

> He that spared not his own Son, but delivered him up for us all, how shall he not with him also freely give us all things? Who shall lay any thing to the charge of God's elect? It is God that justifieth. Who is he that condemneth? It is Christ that died, yea rather, that is risen again, who is even at the right hand of God, who also maketh intercession for us. Who shall separate us from the love of Christ? (Rom. 8:32–35)

2. who teach that God does indeed provide the believer with sufficient powers to persevere, and is ever ready to preserve these in him, if he will do his duty; but that though all things, which are necessary to persevere in faith and which God will use to preserve faith, are made use of, it even then ever depends on the pleasure of the will whether it will persevere or not. For this idea contains an outspoken Pelagianism, and while it would make men free, it makes them robbers of God's honor, contrary to the prevailing agreement of the evangelical doctrine, which

takes from man all cause of boasting and ascribes all the praise for this favor to the grace of God alone, and contrary to the apostle, who declares that it is God "who shall also confirm you unto the end, that ye may be blameless in the day of our Lord Jesus Christ" (1 Cor. 1:8).

3. who teach that the true believers and regenerate not only can fall from justifying faith and likewise from grace and salvation wholly and to the end, but indeed often do fall from this and are lost forever. For this conception makes powerless the grace, justification, regeneration, and continued keeping by Christ, contrary to the expressed words of the apostle Paul: "While we were yet sinners, Christ died for us. Much more then, being now justified by his blood, we shall be saved from wrath through him" (Rom. 5:8–9); and contrary to the apostle John: "Whosoever is born of God doth not commit sin; for his seed remaineth in him: and he cannot sin, because he is born of God" (1 John 3:9); and also contrary to the words of Jesus Christ: "I give unto them eternal life; and they shall never perish, neither shall any man pluck them out of my hand. My Father, which gave them me, is greater than all; and no man is able to pluck them out of my Father's hand" (John 10:28–29).

4. who teach that true believers and regenerate can sin the sin unto death or against the Holy Spirit. Since the same apostle John, after having spoken of those who sin unto death and having forbidden to pray for them (1 John 5:16–17), immediately adds to this: "We know that whosoever is born of God sinneth not [meaning a sin of that character]; but he that is begotten

of God keepeth himself, and that wicked one toucheth him not" (1 John 5:18).

5. who teach that without a special revelation we can have no certainty of future perseverance in this life. For by this doctrine the sure comfort of all believers is taken away in this life, and the doubts of the papist are again introduced into the church, while the Holy Scriptures constantly deduce this assurance, not from a special and extraordinary revelation, but from the marks proper to the children of God and from the constant promises of God. So especially the apostle Paul: no creature "shall be able to separate us from the love of God, which is in Christ Jesus our Lord" (Rom. 8:39). And John declares, "And he that keepeth his commandments dwelleth in him, and he in him. And hereby we know that he abideth in us, by the Spirit which he hath given us" (1 John 3:24).

6. who teach that the doctrine of the certainty of perseverance and of salvation from its own character and nature is a cause of indolence and is injurious to godliness, good morals, prayers, and other holy exercises, but that on the contrary it is praiseworthy to doubt. For these show that they do not know the power of divine grace and the working of the indwelling Holy Spirit. And they contradict the apostle John, who teaches the opposite with express words:

> Beloved, now are we the sons of God, and it doth not yet appear what we shall be: but we know that, when he shall appear, we shall be like him; for we shall see him as he is.

> And every man that hath this hope in him purifieth himself, even as he is pure. (1 John 3:2–3)

Furthermore, these are contradicted by the example of the saints, both of the Old and New Testament, who though they were assured of their perseverance and salvation, were nevertheless constant in prayers and other exercises of godliness.

7. who teach that the faith of those who believe for a time does not differ from justifying and saving faith except only in duration. For Christ himself evidently notes, besides this duration, a twofold difference between those who believe only for a time and true believers, when he declares that the former receive the seed in stony ground, but the latter in the good ground or heart; that the former are without root, but that the latter have a firm root; that the former are without fruit, but that the latter bring forth their fruit in various measure with constancy and steadfastness (Matt. 13:20–23; Luke 8:13–15).

8. who teach that it is not absurd that one, having lost his first regeneration, is again and even often born anew. For these deny by this doctrine the incorruptibleness of the seed of God, whereby we are born again. Contrary to the testimony of the apostle Peter: "Being born again, not of corruptible seed, but of incorruptible" (1 Peter 1:23).

9. who teach that Christ has in no place prayed that believers should infallibly continue in faith. For they contradict Christ himself, who says, "I have prayed for thee [Simon], that thy faith fail not" (Luke 22:32); and the evangelist John, who declares

that Christ has not prayed for the apostles only, but also for those who through their word would believe: "Holy Father, keep through thine own name those whom thou hast given me," and "I pray not that thou shouldest take them out of the world, but that thou shouldest keep them from the evil" (John 17:11, 15).

Conclusion

This is the clear, simple, and sincere declaration of the orthodox doctrine concerning the five articles which have been disputed in the Belgic churches, and a rejection of the errors by which they have for some time been troubled. The Synod judges this doctrine to be drawn from the Word of God and to be agreeable to the confession of the Reformed churches. Whence it clearly appears that some, whom it by no means became, have violated all truth, equity, and charity in wishing to persuade the public of the following perversion:

Namely, "that the doctrine of the Reformed churches concerning predestination, with its associated points, by its own genius and necessary tendency, leads off the minds of men from all piety and religion; that it is an opiate administered by the flesh and the Devil, and the stronghold of Satan, where he lies in wait for all; and from which he wounds multitudes, and mortally strikes pierces with the darts both of despair and security; that this same doctrine makes God the author of sin, unjust, tyrannical, hypocritical; that it is nothing more than interpolated Stoicism, Manicheism, Libertinism, Turcism; that it renders men carnally secure, since they are persuaded by it that nothing can hinder the salvation of the elect, let them live as they please; and therefore, that they may safely perpetrate every species of the most atrocious crimes. And conversely that, in this Reformed doctrine of predestination, if the reprobate should even perform truly all the works of the saints, their obedience would not in the least contribute to their salvation; that this same doctrine teaches that God, by a mere arbitrary act of his will, without the least respect or view to any sin, has predestinated the greatest part of the world to eternal damnation; and has created them for this very purpose; that in the same manner in which the election is the fountain and cause of faith and good works, reprobation is the cause of unbelief and impiety; that many children of the faithful are torn, guiltless, from their mothers' breasts, and tyrannically plunged into hell; so that neither baptism, nor the prayers of the church at their baptism, can at all profit them." And they go on to suggest many other things of the same kind, which the Reformed churches not only do not acknowledge but even detest with their whole soul.

Wherefore this Synod of Dort, in the name of the Lord, entreats as many as reverently call on the name of our Savior Jesus Christ to judge the faith of the Reformed churches, not from the slander which on every side is heaped on it, nor from the private expressions of a few among ancient and modern teachers, often dishonestly quoted or corrupted and taken to a meaning quite foreign to their intention, but from the public confessions of the churches themselves and from the declaration of the orthodox doctrine, confirmed by the unanimous consent of all and each of the members of the whole Synod. Moreover, the Synod warns slanderers to consider the terrible judgment of God which awaits them for bearing false witness against the confessions of so many churches, for distressing the consciences of the weak, and for laboring to render suspect the society of the truly faithful.

Finally, this Synod exhorts all their brethren in the gospel of Christ to conduct themselves piously and religiously in handling this doctrine, both in the universities and churches; to direct it, as well in discourse as in writing, to the glory of the divine name, to holiness of life, and to the consolation of afflicted souls; to regulate, by the Scripture, according to the analogy of faith, not only their sentiments but also their language; and to abstain from all those phrases which exceed the limits necessary to be observed in ascertaining the genuine sense of the Holy Scriptures and may furnish insolent sophists with a just pretext for violently assailing or even vilifying the doctrine of the Reformed churches.

May Jesus Christ, the Son of God, who, seated at the Father's right hand, gives gifts to men, sanctify us in the truth, bring to the truth those who err, shut the mouths of the slanderers of sound doctrine, and endow the faithful ministers of his Word with the spirit of wisdom and discretion, that all their discourses may tend to the glory of God and the edification of those who hear them. Amen.